M000279144

In Love with a Hillside Garden

# *In Love with a*
# Hillside Garden

ANN, DANIEL, *&* BENJAMIN STREISSGUTH

UNIVERSITY OF WASHINGTON PRESS
*Seattle & London*

in association with

THE ARBORETUM FOUNDATION
*Seattle*

© 2009 by the University of Washington Press
Printed in China
Design by Thomas Eykemans
14 12 11 10 09   5 4 3 2 1

All rights reserved. No part of this publication may be reproduced or transmitted in
any form or by any means, electronic or mechanical, including photocopy, recording,
or any information storage or retrieval system, without permission in writing from
the publisher.

UNIVERSITY OF WASHINGTON PRESS
PO Box 50096, Seattle, WA 98145 USA
*www.washington.edu/uwpress*

THE ARBORETUM FOUNDATION
2300 Arboretum Drive East
Seattle, WA 98112-2300 USA
*www.arboretumfoundation.org*

LIBRARY OF CONGRESS CATALOGING-IN-PUBLICATION DATA
Streissguth, Ann Pytkowicz.
In love with a hillside garden / Ann, Daniel, and Benjamin Streissguth. —
1st ed.
    p. cm.
Includes index.
"In association with the Arboretum Foundation."
ISBN 978-0-295-98857-3 (pbk. : alk. paper)
1. Hillside gardening. 2. Gardens—Washington (State)—Seattle. I. Streissguth, Daniel.
II. Streissguth, Benjamin. III. Arboretum Foundation (Seattle, Wash.) IV. Title.
SB458.95.S77 2009
635.09797'772—dc22
2008020379

The paper used in this publication meets the minimum requirements of American
National Standard for Information Sciences—Permanence of Paper for Printed
Library Materials, ANSI Z39.48–1984.

All royalties from sales of this book will be given to the Arboretum Foundation.

# Contents

# Foreword

I T IS EASIER TO WRITE ABOUT ECOLOGY AND THE PRINCIPLES OF environmental stewardship than to dig in and practice them. Daniel and Ann Streissguth have practiced good ecology for decades, without thinking about it and long before the term was coined. They've done it with a garden. Since the 1960s the couple has been making the decisions, one careful plant at a time, about how to cultivate an urban garden that works horticulturally, civically, and aesthetically. And they have done it on a tight site with a steep slope—a very steep slope—that directly overlooks Interstate-5, the busiest and noisiest freeway in Seattle if not the Pacific Northwest.

The garden is a nimble feat of landscape design, spatial packing, erosion control, acrobatic maintenance, and neighborly relations. Coaxing a wheelbarrow full of rocks or soil up and down this embankment requires strength, agility, and mettle. For over a generation, the Streissguths have been steadfast in their commitment to this relatively small piece of land. Including their equally talented son, Benjamin, who grew up working and playing in the garden and is now a professional landscaper, they have beavered away designing, planting, nurturing, redesigning, and replanting their hillside. It requires lots of elbow grease and mental rumination between the bouts of hard labor. This kind of gardening is a robust, not a genteel, pastime.

There has slowly exfoliated on this forgotten hillside a thing of beauty and respect. The Streissguth Gardens are today appreciated as a community asset by a wide audience, thanks to their 1996 gift to the city of the garden's southern section, which they still tend. Neighbors and strangers use the public stairway (or "hillclimb" as it is called in Seattle) that separates the parkland portion of the gardens from the Streissguth house and grounds, which are landscaped with equal thought and sinew.

The story shows how a couple—two busy, distinguished professors—slowly turned adversity (a tangled and inaccessible hillside) into amenity (a beautiful garden). Their tireless effort is an example and inspiration to urban residents who are trying to shape their communities into green, humane places. These citizen-gardeners face the steady assault of traffic and freeways, encroachment and construction, displacement and decay. In this case, it was literally an uphill battle.

Nature, as always, has also done its miraculous part. The plants thrive in symbiosis with one another, with the soil that opens its many dark pores to soft rainfall and with the Cascadian sunlight that is so brief in winter and so prolonged in summer. The vegetation and topsoil sequester carbon, absorbing more carbon dioxide than they release, while providing food and beauty. The garden is also home to urban animals, who enjoy its leafy cover and the vegetables that grow in the raised beds at the bottom of the hill. Earthworms do their slithery and silent tunneling in the top-soil, aerating and enriching it with their nutrient discharge. Birds flit about, attracted by trees, shrubs, and water features. And insects swarm and cross-pollinate the flowers. Competitive harmony, harmonic competition—it is a magical little cross-section of a complex ecology.

This book is not a treatise on urban ecology or neighborhood conservation or landscape design. Rather it is a gentle cookbook and manual about how to intelligently, modestly, patiently, and joyfully build a pleasurable, healthy place in the leftover and unbuildable natural areas of our cities. Providing natural sanctuaries within cities is increasingly necessary as the world becomes more and more urban. (The planet's population has recently become half urbanized and is predicted to be two-thirds urbanized by 2030.) Human comfort and sanity, wildlife habitat, and urban ecosystems demand these sanctuaries. Many of these quasi-public oases will be, like this one, the result of private rather than government or institutional efforts. These bottom-up initiatives will help foster neighborhood goodwill and understanding.

*In Love with a Hillside Garden* is a tale about stewarding a slice of easily overlooked land and about a couple who care deeply about gardening and the environment. It is also a book about personal discipline and the respect in a family for one another and for their neighbors. It reveals the quiet enjoyment and satisfaction that such virtues and the art of gardening foster. In more ways than one, it is a love story.

DOUGLAS KELBAUGH
*Professor and former dean, Taubman College of Architecture and Urban Planning*
*University of Michigan*
October 2008

In Love with a Hillside Garden

# Introduction

I N WRITING THIS BOOK WE OFFER A KIND OF PATHWAY INTO THE hillside greenbelt, which includes the Streissguth Gardens, that is now an entire block of linked woodland paths in the heart of Seattle. We relate how some occurrences in Seattle's development as a city, influenced by the natural terrain of the Pacific Northwest and by chance events in our personal lives, conspired to create a garden, now owned by the city, to which all are welcome.

We describe and illustrate the plants we love, how they got into our lives, how we've nurtured them, and what they've demanded of us. We share our successes and failures in developing a garden on a steep slope with difficult soil but with sweeping, inspiring views of city, water, and mountains. We explain what we were striving for, how we accomplished it, and how you might learn, if you wish, from our experience.

The book portrays the emergence of our gardening partnership during forty years of marriage, and our philosophy of developing a unique hillside site along a well-known public stairway in order to share the garden in meaningful ways with those who pass through. It all began when architect Daniel, then a bachelor, built his own house on a wild hillside lot, eking out a garden that soon encompassed the hillside and natural springs in neighbor Ann's backyard. We married, and together with our growing son, Benjamin, we fought through blackberries, horsetails, and morning glory to push intersecting paths through the adjacent two-lot wilderness we purchased, creating a little park that we planted and nurtured and ultimately gave to the city with our promise to maintain it throughout our lifetimes.

The chapters that follow offer practical insights into our concept of linking inside and outside rooms and of combining public and private spaces. We describe the process through which we transformed a steep forested hillside into a deciduous woodland garden with banks of perennials, a Winter Dell, vistas of the city and lake, and sites for ornamental and food-producing plants. We share techniques we've devised for managing steep clay and sand banks, and spring-fed rivulets and bogs, and we discuss which tools we have found most helpful. We comment upon special collections in the garden and the particular interests and passions of each of us in our gardening activities. Finally, we look ahead, considering the future of this parkland linking the wild and tamed sections of a unique greenbelt garden shared with joggers, strollers, fellow gardeners, schoolchildren, and those who call it "a touch of Eden in a big city." ❀

# Daniel's Guiding Principles in Developing a Garden

❊ A good garden derives from, and must relate strongly to, its topography, orientation, climate, site, and its surrounding bioculture.

❊ A residential garden should be a much-used and beautiful extension to the dwelling of which it is an integral part. It should yield a maximum of pleasure, challenge, discovery, and inspiration through the seasons of each year.

❊ A garden should grow incrementally, reflecting the evolving interests and needs of its users, in choices and arrangements of plant materials and garden elements, necessarily unfolding, changing, refining, and focusing over time.

❊ A good garden demands a continuing involvement and commitment by its users.

❊ Each plant, each element, in a good residential garden should have a substantial meaning to the gardeners. Ideally, there's a tale to be told about every piece of the garden.

❊ A good garden and its house should be a gift to its neighbors. House and garden should integrate gracefully into their surrounds without excessive barriers, and though they should provide appropriate privacy to their users, they should also invite interchange with neighbors and passers-by.

# 1

## The Setting

*Open Space in the City*

ANN AND DANIEL

Buy your house and those jungle lots? You have to be joking! We're just back from being away a year on sabbatical with our baby. We have to get back to our work at the university. But Mrs. Schonacker persisted, and we finally said yes. Out of this small interchange in 1971, a public garden grew.

The Streissguth Gardens (as we now call them) sit on the precipitous steep western slope of Capitol Hill, less than two miles, as the crow flies, from downtown Seattle (figs. 1.1 and 1.2). The garden encompasses four city lots: the East Blaine Street stairway runs through it on a grade too steep for cars (fig. 1.3). As you climb the stairway, our house and garden lie to its north and the public part of Streissguth Gardens lies to its south. Vistas of Lake Union, Queen Anne Hill, downtown Seattle, the Ship Canal, Puget Sound, and the tops of the Olympic Mountains unfold before you, weather permitting (figs. 1.4 and 1.5). From the East Blaine Street stairs, you can disappear into the wooded gardens on narrow dirt paths, finding earliest spring bulbs blooming at your feet or a canopy of blossoms at your shoulder (fig. 1.6). Even from your automobile on Broadway East below, you can look up and see the panorama of color, changing each season as the towering big leaf maples lose or gain their leaves, inhibiting or encouraging the sunlight and the flower carpet beneath.

The landform here, the soils, the plant materials, the geological under-

1.1
Looking northeast from
the Space Needle
toward Lake Union,
Interstate 5, and north
Capitol Hill; Streiss-
guth house circled

1.2
Map of Seattle; vicinity
of Streissguth house
and garden circled

1.3
The first landing on the
public Blaine Street
stairway above Broad-
way East

pinnings of today's urban development, are the products of forces acting
over millennia. In our part of the Pacific Northwest, the glacial activity
of the Pleistocene and post-Pleistocene era formed the land into the distinct pattern of north-to-south ridges and interspersed lakes that now
constitute Seattle. It created, at the southern edge of the continental ice
sheet, a new seedbed that gradually nurtured the predecessors of western
hemlock, which, like the sword fern undercover, thrived in the moist
maritime climate, photosynthesizing even under the local cloud cover.
Douglas fir, with its undercover of salal, preferred the warmer sunnier
slopes.

1.4
Vista looking west from
hillside toward Lake
Union

1.5
The panorama at sun-
set: Queen Anne Hill
and the Olympic Moun-
tains

The original old-growth hemlock and Douglas fir forests of Capitol
Hill were logged around 1870. Big leaf maple began to replace the coni-
fers on the steep Capitol Hill hillsides and in the deep ravines, each tree
producing countless, rapidly colonizing winged seeds. Himalayan blackberry arrived and began to choke out the native undergrowth, proliferat-
ing on the deforested sunny slopes.

Seattle had been founded in 1853. The great fire burned the city's
center in 1893, and the first trains of the transcontinental Great North-

ern Railway arrived that same year. The discovery of gold in Alaska in 1897 eased the great depression of 1893–1896, as Seattle became the gateway to Alaska. As the city expanded to the north, a streetcar line from downtown was operating on 10th Avenue East as far north as East Lynn Street by 1891. In 1900, J. A. Moore platted and began the development of a 160–acre "Capitol Hill" site, with dreams of attracting the Washington State capitol building. Wirth's Addition to the city of Seattle (where our house now stands) had been platted in 1888, including the land between East Howe and East Blaine Streets. The Broadway Second Addition (south of East Blaine Street, where the public Streissguth Gardens are located) was platted two years later, with the street rights-of-way established in a standard sixty-foot width. Much of this narrow strip of land on the steep western side of the hill, between 10th Avenue East and Lakeview Boulevard, north of East Highland Drive, was saved from substantial development by its severe slope (fig. 1.7). The grand homes were built instead in these early years on Federal Avenue East, nearer to Volunteer Park, and along the streetcar line. A section of the steepest, most rugged jungle-like wilderness would much later be designated the "St. Mark's Greenbelt," lying one-third of a mile long immediately south of the Streissguth Gardens (fig. 1.8).

1.6
View of crocus and sword fern along path

In 1903, with the submission of the Olmsted Plan for parks and beautification of Seattle, and in 1909, for the opening of the Alaska Yukon Pacific Exposition, the city engaged in a variety of improvement projects to attract visitors and settlers. The plan for constructing public stairways along Blaine and Howe Streets, in those blocks too steep for automobiles, was approved in September 1909, calling for a standard set of concrete stairways with galvanized iron railing. The stairways were completed in 1911 (fig. 1.9). Along the East Blaine Street stairs between Broadway and the brow of the hill at 10th Avenue East, 90 stair risers, with one walkway and one landing, were built, and from Lakeview Boulevard up to Broadway there are another 203 risers. This two-block

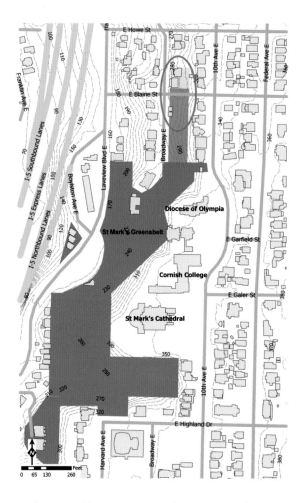

1.7

Contour map of St. Mark's greenbelt; area surrounding Streissguth house and garden circled

stairway is the second longest in Seattle, rising, with its associated ramped sidewalks, 175 feet from Lakeview to 10th Avenue East.

At the same time the stairs were completed, the Lake Washington Ship Canal was begun, to connect Lake Union with Portage Bay and Lake Washington on the east and with the Puget Sound on the west. Six years later the federal government completed the Hiram Chittenden Locks separating salt from fresh water, permitting navigation into Lake Union and beyond to Lake Washington.

In 1910, as the Blaine and Howe Street stairs were being built, approximately 3,300 people lived in what is the present zip-code area of 98102 (west of Volunteer Park, north of Aloha, east of Lake Union, and south of the Ship Canal). Seattle at this time had a population of 237,050, having grown from 80,671 at the turn of the twentieth century.

The first house on Broadway East in the vicinity of the Howe and

1.8
Immediate vicinity map for Streissguth Gardens; Streissguth houses,
private and public gardens circled

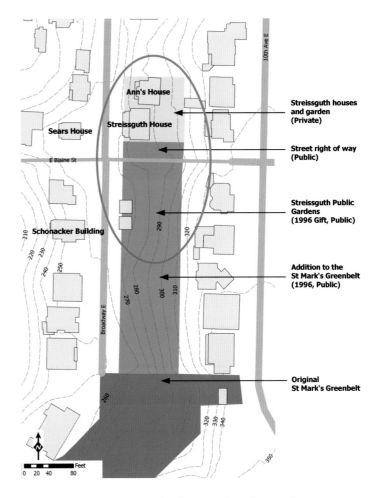

Blaine Street stairs was a "Sears Roebuck House" at the northwest corner
of the intersection of Blaine Street and Broadway East (fig. 1.10). Built in
the early 1900s from an inexpensive house kit available by mail order from
the Sears catalogue, it is still standing. Locals believe that the house, built
before Broadway was graded and paved, was probably served by an early
wooden flight of public stairs predating the concrete stairway of 1911.
Another early structure was the one we know as the Schonacker house,
built facing the Blaine Street stairs on the southwest corner of the same
intersection in 1917. The Schonackers moved this house one lot south,
and physically turned it 90 degrees, in the mid-1920s, presumably to face
the newly paved Broadway East. The Schonackers built garages for their
and their tenants' new cars on their two lots across Broadway from the
house, thus preserving the land on the east side of the new street from
further development. The lot on which Daniel was to build his house was

1.9
Our neighborhood in
1911; East Howe Street
stairway at Broadway
East at the time Broad-
way was paved

1.10
1958 view westward
down East Blaine stair-
way showing the site of
the future Streissguth
house at right (Sears
house shown at top cen-
ter)

1.11
Looking north on
Broadway East, about
1958; Streissguth house
site on right, beyond
public stairway

preserved from early development in being isolated from Broadway, sitting
on a plateau atop the steep thirty-foot cut made in the hillside when
Broadway was paved (fig. 1.11).

The Schonackers' building and the views from this neighborhood had
attracted each of us, independently, as renters, to this surprisingly seques-
tered place in Seattle: Daniel in 1953, Ann in the mid-1960s. Clifford and
Frances Schonacker lived on the top, street-level floor and rented out view
apartments below them to fortunate students and youth (fig. 1.12). During

1.12
Looking south at
Schonacker house in
1955

1.13
West face of Streissguth
house in 1967

our separate tenancies at the Schonacker house, we each grew fond of our colorful landlords. In her heyday, Mrs. Schonacker had been a fur buyer in the Far East for the Hudson's Bay Company; Mr. Schonacker had operated a floating wholesale mercantile company that brought provisions to local stores and saloons in isolated fjords of southeast Alaska. And we loved the old wood-frame Schonacker building, one story high on the east and five stories high on the west, with its views of Lake Union and the city from every level.

Daniel designed his house (fig. 1.13)—now our house—in the late 1950s, while he was living across the street in the Schonackers' building. As a young architect, he had fallen in love with the vacant hillside lot across the street, high above Broadway East beside the East Blaine Street stairway, and he was able over a period of years to put aside enough to purchase it. Design proceeded through several more years, then a construction contract was let in 1960 to the fine Seattle builders Mortimer (George) and Hjelm (Cliff and his brothers, Herb and Elmer). Work was substantially complete in 1961. As the house was under construction, Daniel began the surrounding gardens, conceived as elements integral with the dwelling.

Daniel recalls sitting on the west balcony of the still-unfinished house the day Governor Rosellini's car was the first to drive below on Interstate 5. Although the freeway now enhances our access to the city center and to the entire Puget Sound area, the impact of today's highway roar on this secluded neighborhood and quiet dead-end street, and on our lives, was hard to imagine beforehand.

Sometimes an unexpected event can change one's life forever. That's what happened to Ann when her car broke down on Capitol Hill and she took a walk down Broadway East while awaiting the tow truck. She had recently become an instructor at the University of Washington Medical

School and was contemplating "moving up" from houseboat life on Lake Union to Capitol Hill above, to celebrate the conclusion of her studies. As she walked toward the dead-end of Broadway East, she noticed a "For Rent" sign on a picturesque old frame house from the early 1900s. Mr. Schonacker, the owner, offered to show her the small studio he had available. It was exactly what she was looking for and she took it on the spot. There below her lay the whole of Lake Union with its eastern fringe of houseboats and Queen Anne Hill beyond. She soon fell in love with the steep hillside neighborhood, the rampant woods that extended south, the easy access by public stairway. She also eventually fell in love with her bachelor neighbor, Daniel, who helped her locate the owners of a charming 1920s bungalow perched high on the hill beside his new house, on the uphill side of Broadway East. After renting for a time, she bought the bungalow in 1967. Gardening their backyards brought Daniel and Ann closer together, and in 1968 they married, uniting their gardens. Thus, The Streissguth Gardens began. Daniel's house was the larger, so it became their home; Ann's adjacent house became a rental property where they continue to maintain the garden that Ann began on the hillside above and east of her house.

Our son Benjamin was born in March 1970. When he was eighteen months old, the three of us left for a remarkable sabbatical year encompassing autumn and the harvest season in central Turkey and winter at Daphne Phelps's guest house "Casa Cuseni" in Taormina, Sicily. In Sicily we helped tend the large, terraced Mediterranean hillside garden with Daphne and her helper, Concetta, who provided fine examples, respectively, of English and Sicilian gardening practices. We spent that spring and summer in Gloucestershire, visiting English gardens, observing for the first time in person the great gardens we had only known previously through the books that had inspired our Seattle gardens.

Immediately upon our return, Mrs. Schonacker told us of Mr. Schonacker's recent death. She asked if we'd buy her house on the

1.14
Looking south across the hillside from the Streissguth Gardens to the St. Mark's greenbelt

1.15
Plan of public and private Streissguth Gardens and cross section along East Blaine stairway

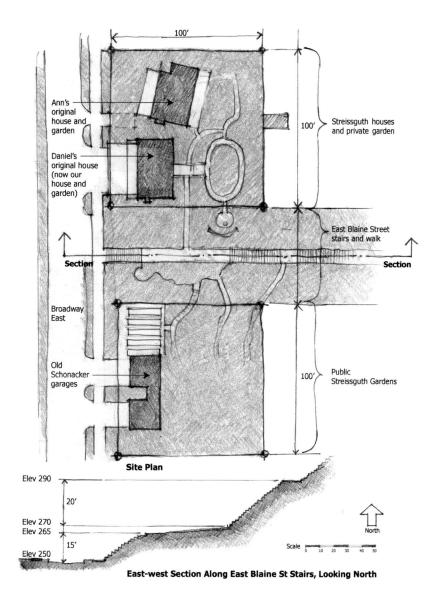

Ann's original house and garden

Daniel's original house (now our house and garden)

Streissguth houses and private garden

100'

100'

East Blaine Street stairs and walk

**Section**

**Section**

Broadway East

Old Schonacker garages

Public Streissguth Gardens

100'

**Site Plan**

Elev 290

20'

Elev 270
Elev 265

15'

Elev 250

North

Scale
0  10  20  30  40  50

**East-west Section Along East Blaine St Stairs, Looking North**

west side of Broadway East. The two lots with the two old garages opposite her house on the east side of Broadway were part of the package; these were later to become the public part of the Streissguth Gardens.

To our eyes at first view, these two wooded hillside lots appeared as a near-impenetrable jungle (fig. 1.14). South of the East Blaine stairs a barricade of blackberry brambles extended where rampant wild clematis vines pulled saplings over into dark mysterious rooms, the foliage masses swinging idly from tall maples. Lush swamps of horsetail (*Equisetum telemateia* and *E. arvense*) sprang up in occasional flat spots where water oozed down from the cool hillside; morning glory fought for a place in the sun; red-tailed hawks nested in the treetops. Nevertheless, after several sleepless nights and visits to mortgage lenders, we made our decision. Yes, we would buy the house and the two steep wooded lots across the street. With this purchase in 1972, the Streissguth Gardens as they now exist were complete in area (fig. 1.15).

Soon after buying the property, Daniel, always public spirited, cleared a little strip of land adjacent to the long, sloping landing on the East Blaine Street stairs. He wanted to beautify the passage a bit. He sowed a lawn there to be a jumping off point to the untamed land beyond. From this foothold, the two of us gradually pushed south into our newly purchased lots, each year chopping a bit further into the wilderness. We built paths (fig. 1.16). We thinned old trees and planted new trees and shrubs, perennials and bulbs. We weeded and grew more vegetables and fruits. After twenty years of this kind of work, we'd pushed the new gardens southward across all the land we'd bought, and eastward from the Broadway sidewalk up to our property boundary forty vertical feet above.

In those years while we were making the garden south of the stair, we thought often of opening it to the public, of giving it to our city. But the small land area, and its discontinuity with any other public lands, made such a gift then seem unlikely and even unworthy of being given. Chance intervened for us, however, in 1990, with the threat of a large condominium complex to be developed on the three heavily wooded hillside lots adjoining our land to the south. We and several hundred neighbors and other concerned people took action, believing the condominium proposal to be grossly out of scale with our delicate neighborhood. We nominated these three properties for purchase by the city in its special program funded by a 1989 bond issue. Its purpose was to secure suitable lands threatened by development, for parks, trails, greenbelts, and other open spaces throughout the Seattle area. To encourage the city's purchase of the threatened hillside, we promised that if the city purchased the three lots, we'd give the city our adjacent two-lot garden on the former Schonacker properties and volunteer our services to maintain it. We envisioned the city's purchase and our gift as safeguarding forever an entire block of new greenbelt in the heart of Seattle.

After a year of monthly meetings of the committee appointed by the mayor to evaluate sites proposed for purchase, ten sites were recommended

1.16
Ben and Daniel build-
ing the first path, the
Woodland Path, March
1975

in late 1994, including the three lots in our neighborhood. When the city completed the purchase of the three threatened lots in 1996, after months of negotiation with the owners, we deeded our two adjacent lots to Seattle's Department of Parks and Recreation.

Our dream of being able to make a significant bequest to our beloved city was realized. The Streissguth Gardens, south of the East Blaine stairway, are now owned by the citizens of Seattle. Everyone is welcome to come and enjoy them; you may find us there gardening. If you do, stop and say hello! ❋

# 2

# Inside-Outside Rooms

*The Streissguth Houses and Their Gardens*

DANIEL

O UR HOUSE (FIG. 2.1) IS BUILT ON A STEEP 54' × 100' HILLSIDE lot. The house "footprint" (24' × 44') was kept small to disturb a minimum of hillside and to reserve a maximum of land remaining for gardens. The house is tall to place the principal floors high enough to capture the superb west outlook and to align the top floor with our existing plateau, the potential best garden for the house, far above the street along the eastern edge of our site.

City zoning ordinances permit two-family dwellings here, so that's what I built. I liked the prospect of rental income helping to pay the house mortgage, and liked the idea of increasing residential density on well-located sites like this, already endowed with great urban amenity.

The house has four stories, each opening onto a section of the hillside adjacent to that level (fig. 2.2). The lowest story aligns with its access street, Broadway East, and provides car shelters and a small basement. The next floor houses the rental apartment, opening to its big outdoor terrace on the roof of the carport below. The third story is the lower, entry level of our house, approached along a brick walk from the Blaine Street stair (see page 2). Our

2.1
House seen from Broadway East during a January 2005 snow; shows newly added house elevator at center of west facade

2.2
The plans of four levels of Streissguth house shown before 2004 elevator installation

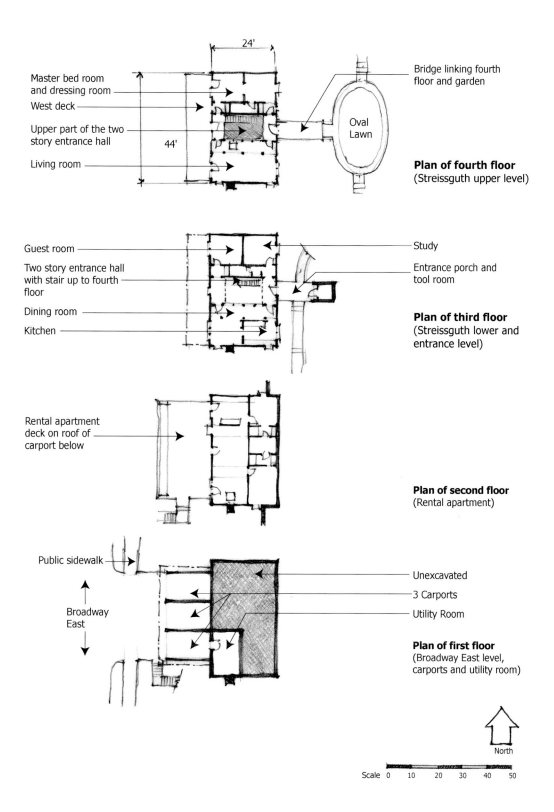

Master bed room and dressing room

West deck

Upper part of the two story entrance hall

Living room

24'

44'

Oval Lawn

Bridge linking fourth floor and garden

**Plan of fourth floor**
(Streissguth upper level)

Guest room

Two story entrance hall with stair up to fourth floor

Dining room

Kitchen

Study

Entrance porch and tool room

**Plan of third floor**
(Streissguth lower and entrance level)

Rental apartment deck on roof of carport below

**Plan of second floor**
(Rental apartment)

Public sidewalk

Broadway East

Unexcavated

3 Carports

Utility Room

**Plan of first floor**
(Broadway East level, carports and utility room)

North

Scale  0   10   20   30   40   50

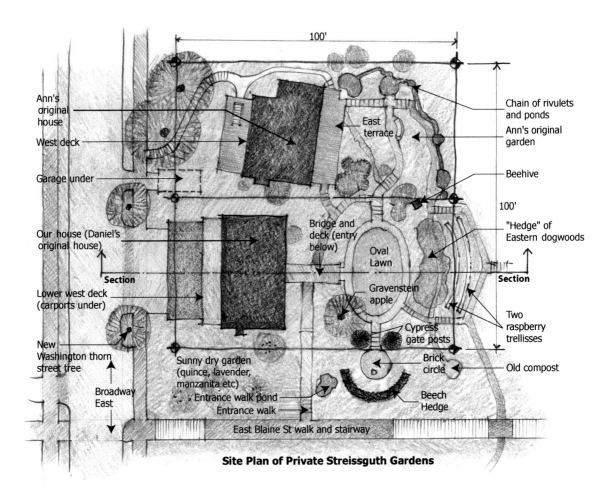

Ann's original house

West deck

Garage under

Our house (Daniel's original house)

Section

Lower west deck (carports under)

New Washington thorn street tree

Broadway East

100'

East terrace

Bridge and deck (entry below)

Oval Lawn

Gravenstein apple

Sunny dry garden (quince, lavender, manzanita etc)

Entrance walk pond

Entrance walk

Cypress gate posts

Brick circle

Beech Hedge

East Blaine St walk and stairway

Chain of rivulets and ponds

Ann's original garden

Beehive

100'

"Hedge" of Eastern dogwoods

Section

Two raspberry trellisses

Old compost

**Site Plan of Private Streissguth Gardens**

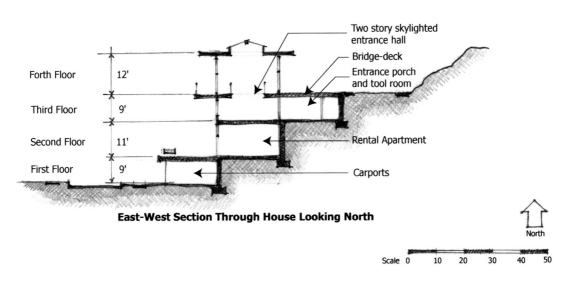

Forth Floor        12'

Third Floor        9'

Second Floor       11'

First Floor        9'

Two story skylighted entrance hall

Bridge-deck

Entrance porch and tool room

Rental Apartment

Carports

**East-West Section Through House Looking North**

North

Scale   0   10   20   30   40   50

two-story, glass-roofed entrance hall is inside, flanked by a kitchen and dining room on the south, and a study and guest room on the north. The fourth floor, the top floor of the house, with the best sun and view, a deck across its west side, houses our living room and master bedroom, and opens to our principal garden to the east.

Our spaces—the rooms of our house and garden—surround and augment one another; they are woven closely and are usable and visual extensions of one another (fig. 2.3). Our daily experiences and our habitable spaces draw from both house and garden. We like preserving the different characters of inside and outside, the distinct experiences each yields. Although discrete wood-framed and mullioned windows and sturdy wooden French doors invite movement and perceptions between inside and outside, they retain a clarity in the differences between the two. There are no "walls of glass" that attempt to blur or conceal this juncture.

At openings in the house wall (fig. 2.4), and at planting enclosures in the garden, we enjoy several kinds of filters, which permit adjustment or change in degrees of privacy, transparency, sound, or air movement. Our windows and doors are usually left fully transparent, open or closed. All our outside windows are operable. Most are double hung, which I like because of their long use in the Seattle vernacular tradition. They permit the outside surfaces to be washed relatively easily from inside. Their necessary vertical proportion allows window heads to be high, admitting light deep into interiors during the gray months, and allows window sills low enough for children and dogs to see out. At outside windows there are tied-back sheer white curtains that can be drawn across the glass if the sun's too bright, and at some of these windows there are creamy translucent roller blinds as well. The west decks are further equipped with adjustable canvas awnings, drawn down on the brightest and hottest days. The garden enclosures are also variable where they exist at edges, and across the sky; deciduous shrubs and trees are leafy in the growing season, nearly transparent in winters.

Within the house, the entrance hall, the two-story sky-lighted room we sometimes call the "winter garden," is overhung by interior balconies from which plants cascade (fig. 2.5). The room's transparent ceiling welcomes sunshine and light into the center of the house, and lets us in the house enjoy colors and patterns in the sky above, changing conditions of

2.6
Garden between house and Blaine Street walkway

2.7
'Tausendschoen' rose
makes north wall of
guest room

2.8
East deck, connecting
top floor of house and
oval lawn

light, clouds, the moon crossing, pattering rain. Adjacent on this level, the dining room introduces through its west windows the outlook and space across Broadway East, extending to the margins of Lake Union below, and to the Ship Canal. The kitchen's east windows overlook our entrance walk, flanked by a bed of white winter-blooming heather (*Erica ×* *darlenensis* 'Silberschmelze'). A near-vertical wall of ivy beyond acts as a retaining structure for the terrace above and becomes a veritable part of the room itself. On this floor, the south windows open out to the strip of land between house and public landing of the East Blaine stairway. Here the garden is kept deliberately treeless to ensure as much southern sun as possible and to link visually the house and public walk (fig. 2.6).

This soil is clay and dry, and we've planted shrubby materials including a number of flowering quinces. We prize two whites: *Chaenomeles speciosa* 'Nivalis' and another which flowers beautifully and is also a prodigious producer of the most fragrant small fruits. Alas, it seems to be no longer in the trade, and we cannot recall its cultivar name; we believe it was called 'Snow Queen'. They scent the entire long sloping landing of the East Blaine stair and are a constant focus of attention in September for walkers in the neighborhood. In this strip we also have planted English lavenders, manzanitas (*Arctostaphylos columbiana* and *A. hookeri*), and additional winter-flowering white heather—all plants thriving in these conditions and of interest to passers-by. We find parents stroking the ripe stalks of the lavender, showing them to their children, searching with their

noses for the quince fruits, or marveling at the sturdy shiny mahogany-colored trunks of the old eight-foot-tall native *A. columbiana*.

Opposite the kitchen and dining rooms on this entrance floor, the little study and guest room also extend themselves through their windows, but are provided greater privacy by large shrubs forming the rooms' termini just outside the glass. Outside one window there is a rampant 'Tausendschoen' rose (fig. 2.7), a years-ago cutting from my parents' garden. At another window, there is a *Camellia japonica* 'Howard Asper', which we prize for its narrow, two-story form and its delicious semi-double rosy blossom. Outside a third window, we enjoy the bushy, multi-trunked, twenty-foot-tall, white-flowered *C. japonica* 'Finlandia'.

Our main floor, the top floor with twelve-foot-high beamed ceilings, includes a living room and master bedroom that open through French doors and adjacent window panels to a continuous western deck. From the sheltered interiors, the rooms' westward enclosures seem sometimes as far away as the summits of The Brothers and Mount Constance in the Olympic Mountains sixty miles distant. In times of heavy clouds, the enclosures are made by the east face of Queen Anne Hill across Lake Union, and in an occasional summer fog rolling in from Puget Sound, the rooms seem to stop at the window glass, the din of city noises muffled and almost imperceptible. On clear nights, these rooms reach out to the twinkling lights of the city and to the glowing streams of traffic on the freeway below us.

The top-floor rooms have direct access to the grassy oval in the highest garden behind the house, via a wood-slatted deck that is actually a bridge and roof over the main entrance door below. The idyllic deck is sheltered by rampant *Clematis montana*, blooming at exactly the time it is first possible to breakfast out-of-doors in early spring (fig. 2.8). Our table

2.9
Luncheon with Daniel's mother, April 1989

2.10
The oval lawn, from the south

2.11
*Cornus florida* encloses
the oval lawn

2.12
*Crocus tomasinianus*,
with dogwoods in Feb-
ruary

2.13
Daylillies in July

then provides a warm, fragrant haven from which to view the jogging activity on the public stair and to enjoy the first rays of morning sun breaking over the rim of Capitol Hill above us.

Beyond this bridge, east of the house, is our oldest and most intensively used garden, our principal exterior living and dining room (fig. 2.9). Even before the house was constructed, this little plateau was treeless and open to the western and southern sun, and it has been kept so for the best warmth, light, and vistas. This is the garden's most architectural place—a brick-ringed oval (fig. 2.10), its shape suggested by the contours of the hillside. It becomes a geometric extension of and contrast to the house forms. This oval is only partially enclosed, by the house on the west, and on the east by four forty-year-old Eastern dogwoods (*Cornus florida*)—more resistant to anthracnose than our native Western dogwood (*C. nuttallii*) and less tall and more spreading at maturity (fig. 2.11). These dogwoods make a blossoming, leafy wall in spring and summer, in autumn a blaze of clear red, and in winter a transparent veil of silvery twigs. Other edges of this oval outdoor room are unscreened and welcome views into the garden and vistas out to the north and south.

The oval room is carpeted with our only lush lawn. It is furnished with relatively light tables and chairs, easily portable and winter-storable. At the perimeter are two teak benches and a mass of aging English lavender, which we used to crop for potpourri but which we still enjoy for its soft silvery colors and fragrance. A 'Gravenstein' apple tree makes a pool of shadow on the lawn, and yields moderate crops (sometimes only in alternate years) of superbly flavored fruit—the very best apple for eating in the hand and for saucing or baking. The bank east of the lawn becomes a carpet of silvery-mauve *Crocus tomasinianus* in February (fig. 2.12). One of our favorite authors criticizes this plant as too easy and too rambunctious; it does surely propagate quickly for us by seed and by corm division. None, however, would argue long on seeing our winter spectacle! Many kinds of bearded iris and daylilies, as well as *Thalictrum aquilegifolium, T. dipterocarpum,* and *T. rochebrunianum,* are all interplanted successfully with the crocus, giving dependable masses of flower in May, June, and July (figs. 2.13 and 2.14). More detailed accounts of these plantings are given in chapter 7.

The oval has changed over the years. Ben's childhood play and friends enriched the gardens for years. When he needed a sand pile, we excavated the oval's south tip to form a lozenge-shaped basin roughly 5 by 8 feet, filled with five tons of sand that we carried up from the street in buckets (fig. 2.15). After many satisfying years of sand pile use, we redistributed the sand to garden paths, carried in new buckets of compost and loam, and the lawn, reconstituted in its original form, reclaimed the sand pile.

The south portal to the oval lawn is marked by "gateposts" of thirty-foot Italian cypress (fig. 2.16). The opening leads to a final outside room, a brick-floored, eight-foot circle (figs. 2.17 and 2.18) embraced by a semicircular, chest-high clipped hedge interwoven of several forms of copper

2.14
Bearded iris in May in the bed above the oval lawn

2.15
The oval lawn with sand pile in 1972; Ben, two years old

THE STREISSGUTH HOUSES AND THEIR GARDENS

2.16
Italian cypress as portal between oval lawn and brick circle, 2001

2.17
Contemporary view of the brick circle

2.18
The brick circle as it was in 1968

beech. We admire the rich metallic reds and the bronzy greens and purples of the beech leaves contrasting with the dominant surrounding greens. One form has matte-textured leaves, another glossy, a third *(Fagus sylvatica* 'Tricolor') has variations of cream and pink. This "tapestry hedge," adapted from those we first saw in English gardens in 1972 (see chapter 6), when leafless provides visual access between garden and public stair. In summer, with plants in leaf, this outdoor room becomes a more private place for suppers, receiving the very last rays of the warm sun before it sets behind the Olympic peaks.

The principal rooms of Ann's original house just north of us open westward to a big deck commanding a great panorama over Lake Union and the city. Two forty-foot Scotch pines at the western edge of the porch have been pruned to permit views through them without topping or removing the trees. The main garden here, however, extends across the steep slope rising sharply eastward and upward from the house floor level. The plantings, which Ann began, and which we together have further developed and maintained, form a mottled tapestry across the hillside, a mosaic wall forming an eastern edge for the rooms facing it (see photo on page v). There is no lawn here at all, but instead a network of brick paths and steps, linking with

2.19
Pond in the garden
above Ann's house

our oval lawn and threading through the dense plantings, paralleling the necklace of spring-fed ponds and streamlets (fig. 2.19) which serve not only to enchant, but also to carry surplus water from the wet hillside.

At one place on the hillside, we've planted a group of camellias. Our two favorites for their November and December blooms are *Camellia sasanqua* 'Briar Rose' and *C. sasanqua* 'Vericolor'. For spring color, we enjoy the previously described *C. japonica*. These give a bit of privacy to the little house's bedrooms. On another section of the moist hillside, we grow a group of hostas, which we treasure for their rich colors and textures. Each one brings unique interest: *Hosta decorata*, with deep veination; *H. sieboldiana*, with bluish-silver leaves, and *H. undulata* 'Thomas Hogg', with white variegation (fig. 2.20). Here also in summer are masses of astilbe—*Astilbe × arendsii* 'Bridal Veil', which is a tall-growing white; *A. × arendsii* 'Fanal', a lovely red with bronze foliage, and *A. × arendsii* 'Ostrich Plume', one of the pinks (see fig. 7.6). We think their drying flower heads continue to look attractive, and we leave them to ornament the following winter hillside. The astilbes are accompanied by billows of our best Shasta daisies (fig. 7.7) and are backed by a towering clump of native goat's beard (fig. 7.8) as a creamy terminus. Giving real piquancy to these assorted whites, pinks,

2.20
Hostas on moist bank
above Ann's house

28        THE STREISSGUTH HOUSES AND THEIR GARDENS

2.21
Euphorbias and
primulas

2.22
Harvested blueberries

and reds, we grow clumps of vibrantly rust-colored heleniums (see fig. 7.9). Bordering the brick walks, we grow the foot-high chartreuse-flowered *Euphorbia polychroma* (fig. 2.21) as an additional color seasoning to the pinks and reds of the dominant astilbes. At the rear of the hillside, on the highest level, their feet relishing the hillside moisture, are our eight blueberry bushes (*Vaccinium corymbosum*): two 'Dixie', two 'Bluecrop', and four whose names we've forgotten (figs. 2.22 and 2.23). We value their splendid fall color nearly as much as we value their prodigious annual crop of the spectacularly delicious, health-giving fruit. We value also the plants' timing of their fruits, coming when we need them after our other soft berries are finished producing, and we value their ability to ripen fruit over a six-week period.

2.23
Blueberries in fall
splendor

Throughout the design of the house and the design and planting of the gardens, the three of us have been strongly motivated to tie ourselves, our residence, and our outdoor spaces closely into the fabric of our neighborhood and city. Dividing our land as it does, and conducting only pedestrian traffic, the East Blaine Street right-of-way (fig. 2.24) has seemed very different to us than a more typical Capitol Hill street carrying both pedestrians and automobiles. We have never felt impelled to separate ourselves from this "street," to wall it off so as to capture a maximum of spaces private to ourselves around our house. Instead, we welcome the interactions we have with our neighbors on the stairs each day. We like to watch them, greet them, and in turn, we welcome offering them the chance to interact with us, to enjoy the gardens we have developed. The gardens around our houses, the gardens on the public street right-of-way flanking the Blaine Street stair, and the now-public Streissguth Gardens south of the stairway, all merge seamlessly. They afford us some shelter and some pockets of relative privacy, but at the same time they settle, we hope softly and comfortably without intrusion, into our neighborhood and on to our hillside.

This, then, is our home. It is composed of the house, or rather the two houses, with interiors so useful and so much enjoyed over half our lifetimes. It is also composed of the gardens, extending and embracing the house, enriching our experiences and nurturing our bodies through each season, maturing and changing as the years unfold. ❀

2.24
East Blaine Street
stairway

# 3

## The Public Hillside Gardens

*Developing a Deciduous Woodland, the Perennial Banks, a Winter Dell, and Combining Ornamentals and Food-Producing Plants*

DANIEL AND ANN

LTHOUGH THE OLDER, MORE PRIVATE GARDENS SURROUNDING our two houses are, in their central parts, principally geometric and regular in form, reflecting and continuing the shapes of the buildings and interior rooms, the new public hillside gardens south of the East Blaine stairway are more incremental, irregular, and naturalistic in their forms (fig. 3.1). Many special physical elements pre-existed at the public garden site, significantly influencing the garden form. A number of different forces and ideas and interests have been interwoven in our shaping and planting of these public gardens. Though many of our design intentions were formulated earlier as we developed the gardens surrounding our house, others have been identified, developed, and refined while we turned the tangled hillside into a garden.

As we began our work in the strip paralleling the Blaine Street walk, Benjamin and his friends, then about four years old, helped with carrying materials (fig. 3.2). We began a kitchen-wastes compost hidden at the end of a short new path. We collected rocks from a midden to free a level bed for phlox starts from Grandmother Streissguth's garden. On weekends we took our machetes and inched forward, bit by bit, until one day in early spring we glimpsed a white flower blooming distantly, faintly, through the heavy foliage. Chomping our way forward to reach the white, which turned out to be a native *Trillium ovatum* (fig. 3.3), we inadvertently

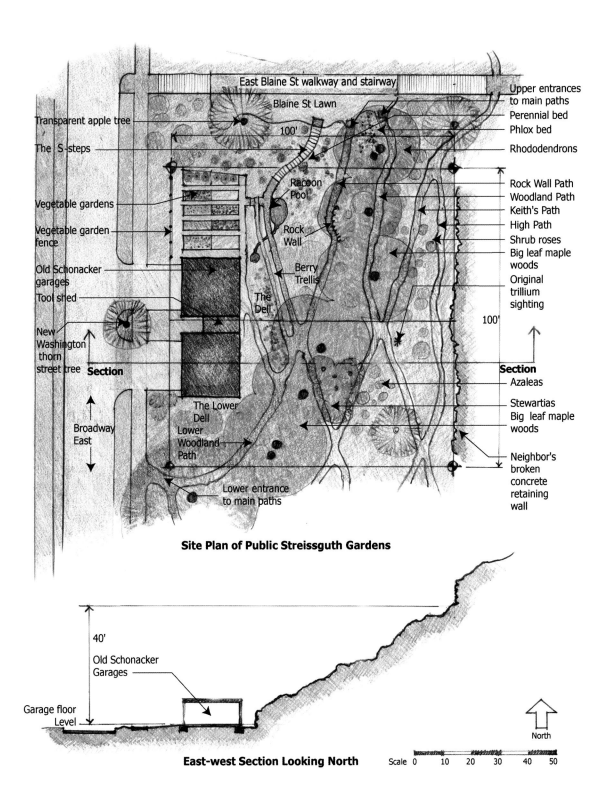

Upper entrances
to main paths
Perennial bed
Phlox bed
Rhododendrons

Rock Wall Path
Woodland Path
Keith's Path
High Path
Shrub roses
Big leaf maple
woods
Original
trillium
sighting

100'

Section

Azaleas

Stewartias
Big leaf maple
woods

Neighbor's
broken
concrete
retaining
wall

East Blaine St walkway and stairway

Blaine St Lawn

100'

Transparent apple tree

The S-steps

Racoon
Pool

Vegetable gardens

Rock
Wall

Vegetable garden
fence

Berry
Trellis

Old Schonacker
garages
Tool shed

The
Dell

New
Washington
thorn
street tree

Section

Broadway
East

The Lower
Dell
Lower
Woodland
Path

Lower entrance
to main paths

**Site Plan of Public Streissguth Gardens**

40'

Old Schonacker
Garages

Garage floor
Level

North

**East-west Section Looking North**        Scale  0    10   20   30   40   50

produced the beginning of the Woodland Path. From that day we were hooked, and many paths followed. How many lovely vistas and shady dells we discovered as the path system grew (it is now about two thousand lineal feet), but never was a flower more lovely than that first trillium.

From here on, in this chapter, we take you on a tour of the public gardens, proceeding upward from the vegetable garden along Broadway East to the high easternmost part of the garden (the High Path) at the top of the property line, near the brow of the hill. Surprisingly, much of this is visible from the street due to the steep grade, especially in winter and early spring before the maples leaf out. Then, we traverse our way back down the slope, first along the East Blaine stairway, then to the southwest along the lower Woodland Path. We end finally at the Dell, the only part of this hillside garden hidden from a viewer on Broadway East. Nestled behind the old Schonacker garages that provide winter protection from our southwest winds, the Dell catches the early morning eastern light of winter under the naked trees to produce a microclimate suitable for some of the earliest bloomers in the garden.

In clearing and beginning to garden the two Schonacker lots, we were like pioneer settlers planning for winter. We quickly designated the flat-test, sunniest ground for a vegetable garden. It sits right at Broadway East. A simple post-and-wire fence stands between the garden and the adjacent sidewalk (fig. 3.4), providing the suggestion of separation from the street (which we feel may be in the best interest of our berries and vegetables),

but providing, too, a conveniently high perch for the elbows of neighbors pausing to pass the time of day with us as we plant, weed, and harvest. The vegetable garden is laid out in five sets of raised planting beds (each set 3 1/2' by 20') that permit comfortable access to the crops by brick-lined paths between the beds, relatively easy to maintain (figs. 3.5 and 3.6). The beds were initially filled with purchased loam and are now renewed each year with fresh compost from nearby compost piles, plus some added cow manure. The beds are double-dug with spades before the spring planting (fig. 3.7). An additional, larger bed has had a mix of 'Quinault' and 'Tri Star' strawberries until we recently replanted with 'Shuksan', preferring the conventional single glorious June crop to the continuous moderate crops of the day-neutral varieties. A high wire fence at the end of this bed accommodates our favorite 'Early Riser' pole beans, with ten-inch flat pods that dry decoratively on the vines in late summer and furnish seed for the next year.

3.4 (top left)
Vegetable garden viewed from Broadway East, winter 1985

3.5
Newly constructed vegetable beds, 1990, and cap of retaining wall

3.6 (bottom left)
Vegetable beds and brick paths, 2003

3.7
Annual double digging

3.8
Egyptian onions

3.9
Tomato houses and "blankies" for vegetable seedlings

3.10
Tomatoes in August (tomato houses no longer in use after 2004)

3.11
Harvest sampler

In our soggy Seattle climate and with less than full sun on the vegetable beds, we prefer to wait until March to plant the early crops of peas, 'Melody Hybrid' spinach, lettuce ('Simpson's Elite' is our best non-bolting producer), and some seeds from Sicily for good luck: 'Quatro Stagione' lettuce, basil, parsley (habitually planted on the north side of tall vegetables to keep it cool), curly endive, and a handful of wild fennel seeds and fava beans that Concetta usually gives us when we leave Sicily. Seeding in annual herbs directly works better for us than buying started plants. Some vegetables, like seed potatoes (always 'Yellow Finn' for their pre-buttered appearance and delicious flavor), and the seeds of dill and arugula, we save over from last year's garden. These we usually plant in March or April, along with shallot and onion starts ('Walla Walla Sweets' and reds do best). For years we grew Egyptian onions (also known as walking onions) as a novelty (fig. 3.8), but finally discontinued them because we seldom thought to harvest them in the fall or winter. Pea ger-

3.12
The slope above the
vegetable garden, show-
ing berry trellis, Rac-
coon Pool, and white
primula

mination, always a problem when planting early, is improved by soaking the peas a day ahead, not planting too deep, and covering seeds with woven glass fiber "blankies" (commonly known as Remay). These coverings permit circulation of air and water, retain some warmth, and keep out the weeds, dogs, and cats. Our earlier experiments with peas were often unsuccessful, but more recently we have had good luck with the variety 'Oregon Trail'.

Summer vegetables go in around the beginning of June, weather permitting. 'Stupice' tomatoes and 'Hungarian Red' and 'Hungarian Yellow' peppers we buy at the Seattle Tilth Association's annual spring garden sale in May and keep in sunny windows until the ground warms up. The single most important factor in having a few ripe tomatoes by mid-July in Seattle (a truly significant gardening goal!) is to use varieties from Eastern European stock, like 'Stupice', with a short growing season. They're not beefsteaks, but they taste great. In earlier years, Daniel built these prima donnas their own wood-frame tomato houses (fig. 3.9), covered with clear plastic, with movable front flaps for easy access (buying greenhouse-quality plastic forestalls annual re-covering). We used a couple of Tomato Boomer fertilizer spikes on either side of each plant, tied the plants up as they grew, pinched out all but a few main shoots on each plant, watered under the tomato houses regularly, and sat back and waited. More recently we're trying tomatoes without houses, to improve the view of the garden panorama from Broadway East, but no sun-lovers are com-

pletely happy in the morning shadow of Capitol Hill (figs. 3.10 and 3.11). Cucumbers and zucchini (seeded right into the ground), bush beans (wonderful luck with the stringless French haricot vert 'Primel') and pole beans, and a little 'Early Choice' sweet corn go in as June progresses.

In July, we replant the pea and spinach beds with rape (seeds from Sicily), Swiss chard ('Fordhook Giant' or 'Vulcan' for the bright red stalks) and 'Detroit Dark Red' beets, which will, unless it freezes too hard, stay in the ground and continue producing until the beginning of the following March. Then it's time to re-dig the beds for spring planting, of course doing a bit of crop rotation for maximum nitrogen production in the beds and to minimize disease. Although our priorities change from year to year (without Benjamin at home, we can dispense with pumpkins), these crops fill our larder and grace our table for most of the year, without excessively preoccupying us or distracting us from the responsibilities and joys of the full gardens (fig. 3.11).

Little terraces on gentle slopes rise above the raised vegetable beds (fig. 3.12). Several hold the Sicilian parsley, basil, and dill. A larger one holds chives, sage, rosemary, and surprisingly, dahlias (mostly tall, cactus-flowered types that seem fairly rain and wind resistant and provide three months of bright summer flowers with very little maintenance and only an occasional winter freeze-out). Fraise du bois, tiny wood strawberries, both red and white varieties (*Fragraria vesca* 'Semperflorens' and *F. vesca* 'Semperflorens Alba'), grow in and around the terraces and paths. Above these, a line of berry bushes, trained on simple, treated 2 × 2 inch trellises, begins and continues diagonally up the hillside, flanked by gravel paths, to link the vegetable tract with the increasingly steep hillside above. Blackcaps (black raspberry) (fig. 3.13) were a gift years ago from our friends Mary and Bob Casey; the fruits have slightly gritty seeds, are a deep purple-blue when ripe, yet are succulently sweet. The arching blackcap canes are extraordinarily beautiful tied to their trellises (fig. 3.14), the surface of each cane covered with a vivid silvery blue-gray, powdery "bloom" in winter. In line with the blackcaps, we've a row of marionberry plants, producing a beautifully flavorful early fruit, and a row of loganberry plants only now reaching their productive maturity. Farther up, along the Rock Wall Path, gooseberries and red and black currants intermingle with perennials and lilies.

Originally we planted the caning berries on the sloping earth between two paths but soon found ourselves unable to keep the plants' roots moist enough on such sharp slopes. Now we've fabricated retaining walls out of treated 4 × 4 inch lumber to hold the soil and water (see fig. 4.4). These planting beds and their rows of caning berries form ascending level terraces up the hillside. Our crops are now much improved, though still limited by too much early summer shade from the maples above.

The Raccoon Pool, the largest of our eight naturally fed, clay-bottomed ponds, is directly above the vegetable garden and the marionberries. It is backed by a dry wall of broken concrete chunks and sections of Wilkeson sandstone. In the wet banks around the pool we grow camass (*Camassia cusickii* and *C. quamash*), fritillaria (*Fritillaria camschatcensis*, *F. meleagris*, and *F. persica*), candelabra and japonica primula (*Primula bulleyana* and *P. japonica*, which move around in giant drifts from one year to another along the moist stream and pool beds), miniature hoopskirt daffodils and the local, native yellow mimulus (monkey flower), which persists year to year, also renewing itself by re-seeding. The "Raccoon Pool" is named, of course, for these many animals sharing the hillside with us. Almost daily we find traces of their having excavated bugs and worms from the mucky soils around the pool. We know they drink from it and probably bathe in it as well. Many times we have tried to introduce tadpoles or juvenile frogs, goldfish, and other fish fry into this pond and others, but the vigilant raccoons prey on every such introduction the very night follow-ing our stocking efforts.

In the other diagonal direction up the hillside from the vegetable garden, twenty-four big paving stone steps in an S-configuration lead to the East Blaine stairway and to our house. On one side, and forming also a garden bank for the East Blaine stairway above, we've planted a mass of mixed daylilies, amongst shrubs like osmanthus of several varieties and shrub roses like 'Bonica' and 'Blanc Double de Coubert' (fig. 3.15), all comfortable on this sunny, clayey slope. Other roses, such as 'Sparrieshoop' and a favorite, *Rosa glauca*, have grown so huge that they have had to be moved farther up the hillside away from the house, where there's more open space. Here as well are 'Reine des Violettes', 'Sutter's Gold', and cuttings we've taken from old floribunda plants from Grandmother Streissguth's garden (she called them 'La Marne'). Also along the S-Steps are the fine *Rosa rugosa* 'Frau Dagmar', prized for her large single flower

and glossy big hips, and our magnificent *R. ×odorata* 'Mutabilis', noted for its fascinating blossoms, some deep pink, others pale cream. It prospers in more sunshine now that a 'Tilton' apricot (diseased in the unsuitable Seattle climate) has been cut down.

Beyond the roses, our sunniest slope, and the one most visible from Broadway, is home for a mass of vigorous, clear yellow *Oenothera fructicosa* and *O. speciosa* 'Siskiyou' from Ann's mother's Oregon garden, and for a concentration of bearded iris. The iris varieties are generally those from thirty years ago, when Daniel began ordering them: 'Great Lakes', 'Broadway Star', 'New Snow', 'Apricot Beauty', 'Maytime', 'Mulberry Rose' (fig. 3.16). All are varieties that continue to be vigorous and are of lovely classic form and color. Still farther south, the slope is more heavily planted with shrubby stuffs: flowering currants, eucryphia, and several tree peonies. The largest of the three flowering currants is a massive *Ribes sanguineum* that creates a cloud of pink in early March. The red *R. sanguineum* 'King Edward VII' and the white *R. sanguineum* 'White Icicle' flower slightly later and slightly below the pink. Our *Paeonia suffruticosa* 'Oriental Pink' adds an astonishing flower in June. Daniel calls the amaz-

3.20
Hillside paths in October (upper left)

3.21
*Nyssa sylvatica* (right)

3.22
Public gardens, October (lower left)

THE PUBLIC HILLSIDE GARDENS

3.23
*Magnolia campbellii*
'Charles Raffill'

3.24
*Romneya coulteri* (upper right)

3.25
*Kalmia latifolia* 'Alpine Pink'

ing flower X-rated. Completing the array of large-scale plantings here are three *Eucryphia ×nymansensis* 'Nymansay', producing a haze of fragrant white blooms in August and September against their dark green, somewhat prickly leaves. The eucryphia, the only evergreen shrubs in this section, do double duty as a year-round loose screen for our oldest working compost pile.

The land above these gardens becomes steeper and woodsier. Here the wandering earthen paths lead laterally and diagonally through the original maple groves (figs. 3.17 and 3.18). The ground cover came to us as English ivy, for which Daniel has a love-hate relationship. What else is such an inexpensive, easy-to-grow, insect-free, evergreen cover? But what else is so invasive, so subject to rat infestations, so demanding of being shaped and cut back so many times a year along so many yards of woodland path and around so many more-desired shrubs? We have for years been gradually reducing the areas of ivy cover, and we have a plan for continuing abatement, but the process will be slow, as will the process of maturing the alternate ground covers. Some of these alternates are discussed in chapter 4. The woodsy paths are as wide as possible, but our steep gradients limit the width of most of our paths to two or three feet. The path edges in these woods are planted—each year we add more bulbs, ordered in the spring from our favorite catalogues as we notice blank places along the paths. The bulbs arrive in the autumn to await the first fall rains for planting: clumps of narcissus, species crocus of every color and dimension, and Star of Bethlehem. Other covers, too, are continually moved over from our older garden to naturalize along the paths for early spring bloom: *Primula vulgaris* (white and yellow from Grandmother Streissguth, and a mauvey-pink that's been there so long that no one can remember where it came from), anemones (*Anemone nemorosa*, *A. blanda*, and *A.* 'Flore Pleno') all multiply freely. Selected self-seeders are also strewn along the paths in the summer and autumn as their seeds ripen, for early spring bloom. These include feverfew, honesty, forget-me-nots and miner's lettuce, as well as some foxgloves (fig. 3.19), which tower above us at seven feet, raining tiny black seeds down our necks as we pass by in the cool shade of summer.

These woodsy gardens benefit throughout from increased sunshine since we removed some primary maples at our neighbors' request. We replaced the maples (which were unhealthy from previous owners' topping) with shrubs and trees of more modest ultimate height, so as not to block the views of uphill neighbors. We chose these new specimens to preserve the sense of a woodland hillside, mostly deciduous plants to ensure a maximum of light and sun in winter and to provide banks of autumn color

3.26
*Rhododendron* 'PJM' and
*Rhododendron lutescens*
'Ashford'

THE PUBLIC HILLSIDE GARDENS

3.27
*Rhododendron* 'Loderi
King George'

(figs. 3.20, 3.21, and 3.22). The stewartia grove includes two *S. pseudocamellia*s (largest flowers, yellow stamens), a similarly flowered *S. koreana*, one *S. monodelpha* (most beautiful exfoliating bark), and one *S. ovata* (flowers centered by a tiny explosion of lavender stamens), all pleasing to look down upon from the upper paths in early summer and all coloring vividly in October.

Our best luck with flowering cherry is the early-blossoming *Prunus × subhirtella* 'Rosea'. We also grow *P. × yedoensis* and *P. × subhirtella* 'Autumnalis', such a favorite in Seattle when the tiny "spring" blossoms appear in December to help one through the darkest winter months. This, the first tree we planted when the blackberries were cleared at the edge of the East Blaine Street stairway, is now hit badly by twig dieback or bacterial blight. We have had good luck with several 'Eddie's White Wonder' hybrid dogwood. These, like our *Cornus florida*, seem only lightly affected by anthracnose, the disease attacking the native dogwood in northwest gardens. Magnolias growing vigorously on our hillside include *Magnolia kobus*, an April cascade of white; *M. sieboldii*, of such lovely branching habit; and *M. denudata*. A more recent addition has been an *M. campbellii* 'Charles Raffill' that Ann gave Daniel on his sixty-fifth birthday (fig. 3.23), despite the fact that our favorite nurseryman, Ned Wells, said we'd never live long enough to see it bloom. Ned felt so sorry for us that he gave us another variety, *M. campbellii* 'Caerhayes Belle', used for street trees in Vancouver, promising that it would blossom at a younger age. Fortunately for us, both are in full bloom in March, their few huge pale-pink flowers almost overwhelming the still small trees: the 'Charles Raffill' is single petaled and classic in shape, her relative more double and paler of hue. We dream of them reaching their full thirty feet to place birdlike blooms high above us in the woodland canopy.

Along the High Path at the top of the hillside there is a collection of sun-loving species and shrub roses, including 'Jacques Cartier', 'Rosa Mundi', 'Erfurt', 'Eglantine', and the lovely 'Hanseat', covered summer-long with large, single, fragrant, raspberry-fuschia blossoms, each with a mass of silken stamens.

At the center of the High Path above the roses stands a beautiful favorite, *Romneya coulteri*, a birthday gift from Ned Wells to Daniel several years ago. Some visitors have likened the flowers to fried eggs. Well, perhaps, but that hardly captures the essence of these delicate, six-inch translucent white petals that are so thin they flutter in the breeze yet support a small golden handful of soft, scented stamens (fig. 3.24). Growing vigorously on five-foot stems from a central clump, they look like hothouse plants, but they require almost no care, little water, and they bloom throughout the summer. Going north along the High Path, one encounters on

3.28
*Chimonanthus praecox,*
wintersweet

the uphill side, under the cherry trees, another carefree, vigorous plant: *Carpenteria californica*. Exotic to Puget Sound but native to the southern California coast, this carpenteria was brought to us twenty years ago by the Wimbergers, celebrating an event now forgotten. In late spring it is laden with single white flowers (three inches across), with yellow stamens. Also on the uphill side of the High Path, nearly to the top landing of the East Blaine stairway, you'll find our collection of kalmias. Perhaps four feet high, they have had several moves in the garden to find their right spot. Judging by their abundant bloom, they are happy now, facing west in the filtered light, covering themselves in clusters of geometric buds that develop very slowly in late spring. One must make frequent visits before discovering the first flowerlet to open. Plants of white, pink, and rose kalmia are intermingled in our garden, but all have the same unique buds, like little umbrellas poised to unfold (fig. 3.25).

Leaving the High Path and proceeding back down the slope into partially shaded areas under the trees, we come to the garden's grand display of rhododendrons. At the north, there is a band of 'PJM' rhododendrons (their strong mauve-violet color is a bit sharp, but we like it, and we love the red-purplish leaf color in winter and the spicy scent the foliage releases when brushed past) (fig. 3.26). Ann plants the clear cool-yellow *Rhododendron lutescens* 'Ashford', with its loose habit and pale pinky-chartreuse new leaves, to provide a touch of lightness to the heavily flowered PJMs. On this same steep portion of hillside, along an upper section of the East Blaine stairway between the walkway and the landing, we grow our collection of scented rhododendrons. We have two of the scented *R. fortunei*, a rangy, loose, tall-growing plant producing heavy panicles of big pearlescent-pink blossoms, spicily aromatic when the sun hits them through the trees. We have also a group of the scented Loderi hybrids (*R. fortunei* is one parent) developed by the renowned English plantsman, Sir Edmund Loder, in the early 1900s: a mature *R.* 'Loderi King George' (fig. 3.27), *R.* 'Loderi Venus', and *R.* 'Loderi Pink Diamond'. Intermixed are the lovely, scented, big white hybrid 'Polar Bear', which is our latest—June blooming—rhododendron, and *R. moupinense*, our earliest-blooming white species. There are, as well, several nonscented pink hybrids that extend the blossoming period, including the spreading low-growing *Rhododendron* 'Cilpinense' *(R. moupinense* is one of its parents), which we find beautiful in January and February but the blossoms seem not reliably hardy through our occasional coldest winters.

In the far southwest corner of the garden, protected by the old garages, a group of deciduous early-blooming species rhododendrons *R. mucronu-latum* and *R. viscistylum* bloom in February and March before their foliage emerges (fig. 3.17). Intermixed are several evergreen rhododendrons (*R.* 'Praecox') that flower at the same time in late February: a mass of pinkish-mauve petals flickering in the filtered winter sunshine

The Dell is one of our greatest treasures, at its peak from January through March. It is only twenty-feet long and ten-feet wide, on the slope above the old garages, in partial sunshine when the leaves are off the maples, and blessed with a pocket of our most friable soil. We visit it daily from September through May. Our plant choices here are influenced by our reading and also by our long enjoyment of the winter-blossoming

3.29
The Winter Dell:
*Galanthus nivalis, G. elwesii,* and *Eranthus hyemalis*

plants in the University of Washington Arboretum collection. Here is our *Viburnum × bodnantense* 'Dawn', a hive of sweetly fragrant pink flowers beginning in December, with two of the exceptionally fragrant *Chimonanthus praecox* (fig. 3.28) and several winter hazels (*Corylopsis spicata* and *C. paucifolia*), which we love for their cool, pale-yellow winter color. The Dell also contains the common snowdrop and the big, bluish-leafed giant snowdrop (*Galanthus nivalis* and *G. elwesii* (fig. 3.29), *Vancouveria chrysantha* and *V. hexandra*, a coptis, hordes of winter aconite (fig. 3.30), jonquils, leucojum, an old double-pink primula from Grandmother Streissguth, and several pulmonaria, all interplanted with *Helleborus orientalis*—the lenten roses (see fig. 6.7). Of the hellebores, we started with one of each: a greenish-cream, a green, a rose, and a deep liver-color. These have now interbred and seeded to form a great flowering carpet in a bed beside our two pussywillows, a black and a French. Originally, the Winter Dell included a *Cornus mas*, but it became so large and shaded so much that we had to cut it down. It had produced a carpet of seedlings beneath its spreading branches, and we have now moved these offspring away to the southernmost, wildest sector of the garden, where their shade is not a problem. There they will burgeon as a new grove and will soon again offer their clouds of tiny yellow flowers in early spring.

All of the woodlands, perennial banks, vegetable beds, and the Dell absorb a big part of our gardening time and capture our intense interest. We visit them often, usually first on our daily garden walks. All the paths here invite public enjoyment, too; they are signaled at their northern and southwestern entrances by basalt blocks inscribed "Streissguth Gardens, City of Seattle, 1996" (fig. 3.31). ✱

3.30
Portrait of *Eranthus hyemalis*, winter aconite

3.31
Basalt block at entrance to public garden path, inscribed "Streissguth Gardens - City of Seattle, 1996"

# 4

## Techniques and Tools

### *Making Gardens Out of Steep Wooded Hillsides, Clay and Sand Banks, and Bogs*

DANIEL

SINCE THE 1960S WE HAVE EMPLOYED MANY HELPFUL GARDENING techniques learned from nurserymen, friends, and family and gleaned from the works of our favorite gardening authors. At the same time, we have invented equipment, facilities, and management techniques of our own—or rather, re-invented them—which have served us well in our rather atypical garden.

Some of our systems have been dictated by the forms of our land, its soil and moisture characteristics, and the plant materials that pre-dated our garden. Our hillside is a product of the glaciers that carved it and deposited its subsoils, of the forests that decomposed into Capitol Hill's thin topsoils. It's a product of land disturbances made by early settlers and woodsmen, and by later street and stairway builders. The ground from our lowest western edge (along Broadway East) up to about the level of our home's entrance hall (the third floor of the building) is relatively pure blue clay. Neighbors occasionally quarry small amounts to try in their ceramic kilns. Above this level, continuing to the highest eastern edge of our holdings, the subsoil is a stratum of relatively clean sand. These described conditions must exist across a substantial part of north Capitol Hill, east of us, as it appears through a year that rainfall percolates through the sand over this large area, until it reaches the top of the clay stratum it can't penetrate. The moisture then runs horizontally along the top of

the clay, reaching the western edge of the hill where we live. There it oozes out in a continuous horizontal band along much of the hill's west face, at a surprisingly constant rate throughout the years. Our high gardens are therefore on sandy, thirsty soils, and our lowest gardens are on nearly impenetrable clay. Our middle gardens can be swamps. We had, in the beginning, only the thinnest of topsoils everywhere.

Our early garden efforts surrounding the houses were at the level of the bogs. As we began taming these watery interfaces, we found foul-smelling black muck, sometimes nearly knee deep, infested with horsetail.

We've invented a system for dealing with these places, involving the cutting of small trenches in the top of the clay stratum, collecting the oozing water into shallow ponds with bottoms nearly impervious to water (fig. 4.1), then conducting the overflowing trickle in clay-bottomed rivulets leading down to a pond (fig. 4.2) at the next lower level, and so on, until finally the stream is conducted into our house drains. Our rivulets are practical, but more important, they are aesthetic. They support a wide range of plant materials along their soggy banks (fig. 4.3). We profit now

4.1
Highest pond and *Chelidomium majus* (greater celandine) in garden above Ann's house

4.2
Lowest pond in garden above Ann's house

4.3
Clay-bottomed pond
beside entrance walk,
self-seeding *Primula
japonica*

from the many light-reflecting basins and from the tinkling of drops of tiny waterfalls as the water descends. This charming sound helps to screen ambient city noises, particularly the rumble of traffic on Interstate 5 just a block below. Acoustic engineers call this effect "acoustic perfume." We benefit in other ways, too, from the moist soils surrounding our ponds, now no longer hopeless mires. Many moisture-loving plants prosper here; the marsh marigold, the greater and lesser celandines, *Primula japonica* (almost too vigorous with its voracious seeding into moist paths), *P. florinda* and *P.* 'Wanda', our blueberries, a ring of ligularia, a bed of water-loving redtwig dogwood (*Cornus stolonifera*), and an annually flowering white water lily, a gift from Benjamin.

Our clay soils we top dress as possible, with the time, strength, and materials we have (usually sands and our organic compost). Generally when we plant in this clay stratum, we excavate the clay to form planting basins, which we then fill with composts and purchased manures. The excess clay is used to make fills along the woodsy paths. We live with the hazard of the clay basins, though filled with good soils, still draining too slowly for many plants we wish to grow.

The sandy soils are easier. To them, we add composts and manures as available when planting, but the biggest difficulty for us has been too-rapid percolation, requiring frequent late-spring and summer watering. In these sandy soils, we form the planting site into large-as-possible level terraces, which permit the pooling of water and prevent erosion down the slopes as we water. Shrubs and young trees, particularly, are introduced in terraces that are deep enough and constructed well enough to persist through the first of several years of growth, until the plants become reliably established and can endure Seattle's usually dry months of July, August, and September. Terraces are partially dug into the hillsides on their uphill sides. On the terraces' downhill sides we use rocks, sod, earth, and chunks of broken concrete laid up in "dry" walls, and also cribbings laid up of treated 4 × 4 inch lumber, as retaining structures (fig. 4.4).

The gardens around our main house are on land that came to us with almost no useful plant growths, only thickets of blackberry, morning glory, wild clematis, horsetail, and miscellaneous seedling trees of various sizes: maples, alders, holly, hawthorn. The high hillside of the public Streissguth Gardens came with a heavy ground cover of feral English ivy and fountainlike tangles of mature, foot-thick suckers from stumps of big leaf maples lopped off long ago by others. The ivy we live with, though the truce is uneasy. We've adopted a gradual process of ivy abatement and are actually using as replacement covers such natives as sword fern, Oregon grape, kinnikinnick, our two vancouverias, the Pacific Coast iris,

4.4
4 × 4 inch cribbing
holds loganberries
above the Dell

and the ubiquitous tellima. Of non-natives, we find useful *Epimedium grandiflorum*, *E. × rubrum*, and *E. × versicolor* 'Sulphurium', omphalodes, comfrey, *Anemone blanda* and *A. nemorosa*, sweet woodruff, and cyclamen. We've removed perhaps half of the maples and have radically thinned the other clumps. Our former neighbor, John Mailhiot, is a skilled arborist. Each year we employ him to remove selected trunks that are diseased, that block views from above, or that generate too dense a shade cover. He also cuts up the many small side shoots in healthier specimens, "limbing up" the trunks so that we can enjoy tall, relatively open, columnar trunks, through which the upper neighbors' views prevail. The untopped crowns spread beautifully against the sky (fig. 4.5).

In a different garden sector, we engaged John to pollard our four London plane street trees along Broadway East, removing all the previous year's vertical suckers and pruning the tree structures into lovely umbrella shapes that arched over and shaded the street below. The planes were a mixed blessing. Although we loved the dappled light on the street, and the massiveness of their mottled gray trunks, flecked as chunks of bark dropped off, we regretted too much the need for substantial annual maintenance, the planes' great mature size and scale, and the tendency of their roots to heave sidewalks and invade drain lines. In 2002 we had the trees cut, grieving at their loss and the resulting barrenness of our access street. Benjamin installed as replacements five young Washington thorns, which we hope will stay at a more appropriate size for our narrow street. They require

4.5
Thinned, limbed big-leaf maples in public gardens

4.6
Berry trellises

less maintenance than the plane trees and give a splendid autumn color.

Ben works with us each year in shrub and fruit-tree pruning. He has a fine eye for optimizing and keeping the beautiful structural form of fruit trees while maximizing their fruit production. In addition to our magnificent thirty-five-year-old 'Gravenstein' apple, we have a younger 'Yellow Transparent' apple, a 'Bartlett' pear, several flowering crabs and plums that produce smallish, usable fruit, and the fruit-bearing quinces described earlier. We also have patches of caning berries, from which we prune out the old growth each autumn, training the new canes onto simple T-shaped, $2 \times 2$ inch wooden structures (fig. 4.6) that support next year's crop at picking level (see also figs. 3.12, 3.13, and 3.14).

Composting has been with us throughout all our gardening years. We now operate five big piles. The one nearest our kitchen receives all our fruit and vegetable parings. We do not compost meat, cheese, or table scraps, finding that they attract rats and neighborhood pets. All garden clippings, pulled weeds, raked leaves and duff, even small twiggy residues and fireplace ash, are composted. Our composting is perhaps not typical. We generate so much material for composting that Daniel hasn't strength or time to turn frequently and properly aerate the piles. Neither is it necessary to water the composts, as the Seattle climate provides sufficient moisture. Instead, we stack the compost ingredients carefully and let our millions of red worms turn each year's leavings into next year's soil. Then we harvest the new soil and distribute it where most needed to nurture the gardens' plants (fig. 4.7). Each compost pile yields perhaps twenty full wheelbarrows each several years. Several of the piles are in excavated basins. Others rest simply on existing ground surfaces. One pile is reserved for larger woody residues—they take even more years to decompose. Woody pieces larger than a couple of inches in diameter are cut into firewood and stored in piles under our house eaves, along with the regular maple logs harvested in our pruning and thinning efforts. Stacks are self-supporting and kept about a foot clear of the wooden house walls. We clean the space between wall and stacks annually, which helps to discourage carpenter ants and other vermin from homesteading.

We try to construct our landforms and garden structures in ways we can manage by ourselves, using shovels, wheelbarrow, and hand tools. We rely as little as possible on mechanical earth movers and tools, purchased concrete, or imported labor. (We do enjoy, however, a small electric chain saw and electric hedge-clippers.) Our hillside paths, like our planting terraces, are made by cutting into the uphill side with a shovel, distributing the excavated soil on the downhill side, then healing the verges by re-shaping the existing ground cover, planting pathside bulbs and new ground covers, and preventing erosion and suppressing weeds and retaining moisture on the raw downhill side with heavy layers of decaying maple leaf compost from the year before (fig. 4.8) The vegetable garden and some of the berry plantings growing on hillside slopes have benefited greatly from the construction of raised beds and retaining structures of treated $4 \times 4$ inch lumber. (The WSU Agricultural Extension service advised that "treated" materials are safe for use in kitchen garden areas.) We connected the timbers with long galvanized nails, and we pounded vertical retaining "stakes" of half-inch metal reinforcing bars into the clay subsoils. By conserving water and fertilizers at the roots of berries with these raised beds, we have doubled our berry crop (see fig. 4.4).

Our tools are important. We try to have the best quality possible, but even among these fine-quality items we find substantial differences in dimensions and adaptability to our respective physical dimensions and working styles. It's great to have on hand exactly the right device, without borrowing from a neighbor or making the trip to a hardware store. We

4.8
Newly constructed path in public gardens, 2002

began with only a few tools but gradually find ourselves equipped with
quite a number. All of them come into use during a garden year, but they
are rapidly outdistancing our tool-room storage space. A complete list of
the tools we use, indicating those we consider indispensable, appears in
Appendix 1.

Summertime watering has tested our ingenuity. In keeping with our
inclination to keep our garden efforts on a scale we can ourselves construct and manage, we have not installed sub-grade irrigation systems
anywhere (often we sorely regret this decision). We rely instead on large
numbers of hoses (we have probably thirty of the fifty-footers), which we
leave in place along the garden paths during each watering season, conducting water from taps at the house to the far corners of the garden.
From past dry years, with restriction of sprinkler use during the summers, we have accustomed ourselves to much hand watering. On the one
hand, this is time intensive and is possible now only in Daniel's retire-
ment (fig. 4.9). On the other hand, it is water efficient, directing the
water only where it is needed, onto the thirstiest beds and into the driest
planting depressions, and not watering ivy ground covers, not nourishing
weed seedlings in the paths, and minimizing the occurrence of mildew
on leaf growth. Only in the driest summers now do we use occasionally
our portable, long-stemmed rotary overhead sprinklers on lawns, or to
refresh too-dry hillside sections when hand watering seems inadequate
to cope with drought. In recent years, our water use is only about half

TECHNIQUES AND TOOLS

or two-thirds of what it was when we relied mostly on overhead sprinkler irrigation. We enjoy, as well, a consequent saving in waste-water disposal costs (which in Seattle are linked directly to water consumption, without regard to whether the water consumed goes into the public sewer system or is distributed onto the land).

In former years, our neighbors above us on 10th Avenue East kept hives of bees, but they no longer do so. Missing the presence of these attractive creatures, and missing the fruit that the bee's pollinating actions helped, Benjamin gave the garden several of the little wooden hatcheries for mason bees. Adults emerge just as the apple blossoms begin to open, then later in the season the masons return to the same holes to lay eggs for the following season. Masons do not store honey, but they are early and vigorous pollinators. Even more generously, Ben gave us a combined mother's and father's day gift several years ago: a hive of honey bees, including his offer to maintain the hive for us (fig. 4.10). We're amateurs, but the bees produce some delicious combs of honey, presumably from Streissguth Garden flowers. Ben is experimenting with keeping the hive healthy and with feeding the bees enough, early in the year, to nourish them until they develop their own food sources. While we look forward to years of honey-laden tables and well-pollinated crops, we're well aware of recent beekeepers' problems with diseases and parasites and ourselves have lost several hives in several winters.

Formerly we used herbicides to rid paths of unwanted plant growth and to kill some persistent pests, such as wild clematis, morning glory, and Himalayan blackberry. But we have found the cost of their use, in terms of the suppression and destruction of desired plant materials, to be too great. We now rely on manual measures of weed control. We use fewer and fewer pesticides, though we still feel we must protect many of our emerging seedlings and new transplants from our voracious, prolific slugs and snails (fig. 4.11); Corry's powdered slug-bait seems most convenient and effective. We also find we must spray some of the older varieties of our roses against mildew and black spot in order to have any blossom or foliage growth at all, but we try to do this minimally and selectively. Many of our roses are relatively disease resistant, for example, *Rosa rugosa*, *R. × odorata* 'Mutabilis', and *R. spinosissima*.

4.11
Snails

I wish I knew of a spray I could use to protect our extensive lavender and campanula plantings against spit bugs. My daily flushings by hose haven't helped at all—the bugs are back the next morning—and I haven't found the old wives' remedy of soapy water useful, nor have I found effective any of the more potent insecticides I keep closeted in our tool room. Manual squashing is out of the question, as we have literally thousands of spittle-festooned flower heads in a season.

We use a great deal of organic fertilizer. Dried chicken manure is slightly more potent than dried steer or cow manures. This we buy in garden-center sacks rather than in bulk, as sacks are easier to haul in our station wagon and to carry on our shoulders up stairs and steep hillsides. Even better, Ben now brings us pickup truckloads of composted cow manure from a Snoqualmie Valley dairy farm. The splendid stuff is stored in a discrete pile at street level and carried in galvanized buckets to hungry plants on the hillside above. We've also found the Osmocote fertilizers to be wonderful in their timed-release quality, if rather costly, and we now use them extensively, especially in the vegetable garden.

Weeding is, of course, the most used of all our gardening techniques. It is the gardener's unending and most exhausting work. Among the bad plants we weed out endlessly are chickweed, dandelion, maple and wild clematis seedlings, thistle, and annual grasses. Worse are those even bigger and wider-ranging invaders, such as Himalayan blackberry, morning glory, quackgrass, horsetail, and nettles. For those, control takes a number of years of consistent, repetitive work. We control the blackberry by digging out the knotlike root structure beneath the soil level. Horsetail we conquer gradually by pulling all new shoots as they appear, particularly the spore-filled male heads. The worst weeds of all in our garden are morning glory and rhizoming quackgrass. We had found no successful eradication technique for these until last year, when Ben wiped out several patches by cutting them back in the autumn and covering them with half-a-dozen or so layers of newspapers, on top of which we piled maple leaves from our canopy. Nine months later we were able to replant the areas and begin weeding out any new shoots that appeared. Prior to this, we dealt slowly and unsuccessfuly with the problems these plants posed, pulling each green shoot as it emerged in the hope of eventually starving the fleshy roots. Trying to dig out these wanderers seemed only to divide them into several still-vital pieces, each of which formed a new plant.

4.12
Weeding with bushel
basket

There are ways to ease this work. A good basket is a blessing (fig. 4.12). Knee pads are a great help to me, as I prefer weeding on hand and knee. Mulches help greatly in suppressing weed growth, hoes are useful to spare the weeder's back, vigilance in pulling blossoming weeds before the seed is released is a great assist, but perhaps the best remedy of all is the encouragement of desirable ground covers. We permit mosses in many places. We enjoy pampering small plants such as creeping phlox, dwarf campanula, carnations, anemone, and cyclamen. We assist Corsican mint and common babies' tears as easy covers. We love forget-me-not and permit many violets (though we eradicate the pink-flowered form which we find too invasive). We encourage seedlings of the Alpine or wood strawberries everywhere, but we relentlessly weed out a new (to our garden) creeping variety of invasive non-fruiting strawberry that has only appeared in the past five years. We also weed out a yellow creeping jenny that we unwisely let go too long, after it hitchhiked in from Ann's mother's garden.

A final word on weeding: although it is ever present and very heavy work, its constant demands are one of the best reasons to be in the garden over the days and months of the year, in the freshness of morning, the warmth of midday, and the lovely light of late afternoon. Weeding provides the satisfying touch of hand to earth and produces one of the garden's most immediate and intense satisfactions when the gardener surveys a just-weeded section, sure of the very positive worth of the hard work just completed. ❀

# 5

## Plants Who Do Their Share of the Work

ANN

ONE OF THE STEPS WE'VE TAKEN IN TAMING THE HILLSIDE for a garden involves the early use of plants that reproduce freely and with great abandon. Clearing out undesirable plants is fruitless if the open spaces aren't soon filled with plants chosen to sustain the gains made and reduce the rate at which the weeds return in subsequent months and years. Several types of plants have been most useful as we've forged our way across the hillside, path by path: plants that are prodigious seed producers whose seeds germinate easily in the Seattle climate and whose seedlings are not overwhelmed by weeds; plants that grow easily from cuttings that can be tucked in here and there in rock crevices or along the woodland paths; and plants that spread spontaneously from rambling roots, underground runners, or self-dividing bulbs.

We recognized the value of the money plant and feverfew as they emerged spontaneously on the hillside when the thickets of blackberries were first cleared. Money plant was already growing abundantly on the wild hillside, cohabiting with English ivy under the canopy of the old maples. This is truly a plant for all seasons. We enjoy the vigorous pointed green leaves of the first-year seedlings

5.1
*Lunaria annua* (money plant, or honesty)

58

bravely raising their heads above the ivy cover, and the bright purple spring flowers of the second-year plants (fig. 5.1) competing handily with other flowers requiring ten times their care. Finally, in their maturity and final demise in the autumn of their second year, their lovely translucent seed membranes hang like tiny moons from their branching arms, gradually blessing the surrounding earth with their promise of life (fig. 5.2). After the seeds are spent, and before the ravages of the winter rains begin, what lovely long-lasting bouquets this money plant makes; what luminous ghosts the remaining plants become in the woods in winter, gradually giving way to the next crop of first-year seedlings.

Feverfew, though more conventional in habit, is another favorite (fig. 5.3). Seemingly impervious to our Seattle seasons, this plant germinates throughout the year, so that young plants with their tiny white flowers provide soft feathery drifts across swaths of hillside and along garden paths in spring, summer, and fall. The spent plants are easily uprooted and the seeds shake naturally from the plant while we walk along the woodland paths. Feverfew grows with such profusion yet is so easy to control that it makes an excellent "first pass" planting in areas that will, after taming, be receiving more difficult plant materials.

Raggedy robin, with soft silvery leaves and bright cerise flowers, is another old friend who has helped us tame the woods (fig. 5.4). These biennials prefer the sun, but they are freely seeding and spreading and can also be sown directly from uprooted plants in autumn. Although

5.2
Money plant seeds

5.3
*Chrysanthemum parthenium*

5.4
*Lychnis coronaria* (rag-
gedy robin)

5.5
*Digitalis purpurea* (foxglove) in front of Solo-
mon's seal (*Polygonatum
biflorum*)

friends keep giving us the white variety, it seldom multiplies for us like the cerise form. Foxglove is another prolific seeder. Its scale is perfectly suited to a large wooded hillside like ours (fig. 5.5), and the lofty spikes contain dozens of tightly packed hanging trumpets that are perfectly shaped for children to wear on their fingers like gloves. These flamboyant giants place themselves here and there on the hillside, sometimes growing in the ivy, other times along the paths. Foxgloves can generate profound thoughts as you contemplate the miracle of reproduction they represent, by growing from a seed the size of a period to a strapping plant of seven feet in only two seasons. We particularly enjoy the many different colors that emerge in each year's family of foxgloves. From darkest mauve to palest pink, and even pure white, they grow elegantly throughout our hillside. Our opinion, of course, is not shared by all. We still recall one friend touring the garden with us who exclaimed in horror, "You don't let *those* grow here, do you, they're nothing but weeds!" As our old gardening friend, Daphne Phelps in Sicily, always says, "A weed is just a flower growing in the wrong place."

Several types of plants reproduce readily by cuttings, which can be pinched off either in early spring or when the fall rains begin. These have been of great help in bringing winter and spring color and form to the hillside gardens. Some of our favorites are the ground covers that bloom with the spring bulbs. A full border along the S-Steps and fifty feet of planting beds in the retaining structures under the caning berries were planted with pink and lavender aubrieta, snipped from existing garden plants. We treat arabis the same way, often pinching off bits and tucking them into rock walls as we walk along the garden paths with friends. Old-fashioned dianthus, soft pink and rose helianthemums (*Helianthemum* 'Wisley Pink', *H. nummularium*), and low-growing white rockrose are all plants that are easily started by cuttings set straight into the garden after the plants bloom, when a heavy clipping back can sometimes produce a second burst of late summer flowers (some discretion in water and shade is necessary if this is done in the heat of summer). Winter jasmine produces a tangled web of stiff bright-green vines that is particularly useful in steep hillside areas with poor sandy soil. This plant grows effortlessly from twigs stuck into the ground in autumn. The following year after the leaves are gone, small brilliant-yellow single flowers appear, their fresh faces producing tiny surprise bouquets in midwinter.

Equally useful are the ground covers that spontaneously form large clumps. These can readily be divided to produce broad swaths of spring bloom or to give to friends. Large beds of *Primula vulgaris* (fig. 5.6), after several seasons of initial weeding, now stave off many weeds singlehand-edly while simultaneously producing showy displays of cream or yellow, depending on their destiny. Larger plants, such as astilbe and our several perennial geraniums (*Geranium himalayense* and *G.* 'Johnson's Blue'), also dampen weeds and bloom vigorously in early summer.

Finally, there are the plants that reproduce themselves with absolutely no work at all on the part of the gardener, beyond planting them in the right spot. Our lovely clear-yellow oenothera, which languished in our shade garden, perked up immediately and spread itself across an entire hillside once we moved it into the sun. This *Oenothera fruticosa* (fig. 5.7), like our native fireweed, spreads underground with rapidly extending roots. It is moderately invasive but not as free-ranging as fireweed. The tight mass of leaves and roots produced by *O. fruticosa* is particularly useful in

5.6
*Primula vulgaris*

5.7
*Oenothera fruticosa*

weed control. Another plant, leopard's bane, is *not* a bane to gardeners—it also spreads happily in space available, keeping weeds and ivy at bay and sending up abundant two-foot stalks of large bright-yellow nodding flowers. Lily-of-the-valley, so fragile seeming in early spring, is another rampant spreader that can be useful in some spots but a problem in others.

5.8
Gooseneck lysimachia

5.9
*Galanthus elwesii*

Hillsides as large as ours can even accommodate a lovely patch of fireweed, especially when it cohabits successfully with ivy to produce a mass of summer color. We attempted many times to bring fireweed seeds with their soft downy covers home in our pockets from mountain hikes. We'd release them to float through the woods, but they never "took." One day, to our great surprise, we found a tiny fireweed plant growing spontaneously in a flower pot at the house of some friends. They happily gave us the plant and pot, and we carefully transplanted our fireweed baby to a sunny spot along the High Path in the woods just as the rains began. This became the founding parent of a little plantation of fireweed that is a pleasant surprise in a city garden. Gooseneck lysimachia (fig. 5.8) is another busy spreader, rampaging through our summer perennial bed adjoining the oval, a bed it is supposed to be sharing with liatris, filipendula, and monkshood.

Iris, of course, are also wonderful spreaders, but the bearded hybrids require much time and effort in resetting to avoid the spreading masses of tangled tubers that soon decrease bloom. We are now experimenting with some old-fashioned varieties, the kind we see growing in huge clumps at abandoned houses in Sicily, blooming their heads off with no care at all, and no dividing, even years after the last resident has left the premises.

Several types of bulbs also fall into the category of plants that reproduce easily from seed or by producing a profusion of bulblets. Earliest in the spring come the snowdrops, first the sturdy *Galanthus nivalis,* then *G.*

5.10
*Crocus tomasinianus*

*elwesii* (fig. 5.9), which years ago we began planting in little clumps of six or eight. After several years, they began multiplying vigorously, drifting downward in cascading carpets of white on sunny slopes where they open surprisingly around Valentine's Day. Unlike many other earliest flowering bulbs that hug the ground, snowdrops hold their little bells on dainty stalks that let them dance in the passing breezes.

Early winter aconite is also self-seeding, but in our garden it grows best in flat places and doesn't like being disturbed. After a number of years, when the plants mature, they begin spewing seeds all about them. It takes three to four years for the new seedlings to begin flowering and gradually to create an ever-expanding patch of yellow as bright as a shaft of sun in February. Numerous child visitors to the garden have marveled with us at the successive age-related examples of aconite genealogy visible in late spring and summer: first-year seedlings are the dicotyledonous, with two opposing leaves; second-year offspring have a small ruff of lacy green leaves; by their third year, they are sturdy adolescents with large encircling green ruffs ready for next year's flowers.

The spring blooming *Crocus tomasinianus*, mentioned in chapter 2, produces huge drifts of pale silvery-violet translucent flowers in late February (fig. 5.10). They reproduce by corm divisions but also by a burst of seed from a substantial shaft that first appears among the grassy leaves after the flowers fade. In the warmth of early summer, the leaves die back to fully expose the seed shaft, which drops large pale-tan seeds around itself to form tight clumps of new seedlings, just the right size for a spadeful for a visitor, or to move to another location. Eventually growing together into impressive seamless drifts, these species crocus don't mind being disturbed. In fact, they often begin colonizing a whole new area of the garden from a single bulb or two that hitchhikes to another part of the garden when another plant is moved.

The small species *Cyclamen hederifolium* produces a textured carpet of dappled leaves most of the year, gradually dying back in the heat of summer. As the first rains come in early autumn, perky bright-pink and occasionally white flowers bloom from large corms that look like slabs of old leather lying atop the surface of the earth. The corms not only con-

tinually increase in size themselves but also produce an increasingly large number of flowers that set their seeds in fat pouches perched on the end of tightly coiled springs. In early spring, before the dappled leaves appear, the springs release, the pouches burst, and the seeds are ejected in all directions across the surrounding territory. The original plant, a gift to Daniel thirty-five years ago from Jane Campbell's Port Townsend garden, has now multiplied to a bed nearly as broad as the canopy of the 'Gravenstein' apple tree, under which it thrives (fig. 5.11).

Not all vigorously spreading bulbs delight us, however. Squill (*Hyacinthoides hispanica*) is an example of a real pest. These must not be confused with their more constrained relatives, the English bluebells (*Hyacinthoides non-scripta*), which form lovely clear blue carpets in hardwood forests of western England; or with *Scilla siberica*, the tiny, reticent flower of luminous aquamarine blue that is so vulnerable to slugs in our borders. By contrast, squills rampage out of control on the upper reaches of the hillside, not the least intimidated by ivy or anything else in their way. These squills with their muddy blue flowers predated our entry to the hillside gardens and have made such massive settlements that it seems beyond our collective abilities to remove them. Right now, we'll call it a victory if we can keep them from spreading into new areas.

Wallflowers, linaria, Welsh poppy, and larkspur are all useful easy seeders on the hillside, varying immensely in virility and adaptability. Our favorite violets include *Viola labradorica*, *V. riviana*, *V. sororia*, and *V. tricolor*.

Wallflowers are just plain comfortable to live with. They come in a broad range of rusty brown to yellow hues, spontaneously set themselves into crevices in rock walls that no other seeds will attempt, and reward all passersby with their sweet spring perfume. Wallflowers, like linaria and violets, seed in easily, but are also easy to weed out.

Larkspur, like feverfew, germinates at many different times of the year, as long as it gets some moisture. Her clear blue flowers are among the truest blues in the garden, though she doesn't compete well with other plants and is rather a free spirit, seldom returning where she last was seen. You must be careful to gather seeds every year (so you can get this plant started again if it didn't like where you put her last year). I snip off the seed heads just as they're ready to open, then I let them finish drying inside, in a pie tin, as the seed is quick to disperse when ripe and won't germinate if it falls into a dense cover. When the seed is dry, I winnow off the chaff by blowing lightly across the top of the tin until only seeds remain. As with all my seeds, after winnowing I store them without further fuss, in long envelopes with name and year, ready for distributing along the garden paths when conditions look right or to give to visiting gardeners.

Welsh poppies are almost irresistibly showy and flirtatious with their nodding clear-yellow translucent heads (fig. 5.12), but they spread so rapidly throughout the garden that they overwhelm weaker plants. Their long tap roots make them a significant problem to weed out, especially as they get more firmly entrenched. I can still remember the look of amusement on the face of an old nursery woman at a country primula farm that we visited about twenty-five years ago. We bought a few primroses, and when I asked her if we could also buy one or two of her lovely Welsh poppies, she said: "Oh, I don't think you'd want those. You'll never get

5.12
*Meconopsis cambrica*,
Welsh poppy

rid of them once you get them started." Looking about at the lovely drifts of yellow poppies blooming along her paths and streams, I simply didn't believe her and could hardly wait to start them in our gardens. Well, we did, and they are flourishing and they are beautiful, both when their soft, lacy lime-green leaves appear in spring and when they bloom throughout the spring and summer. Throughout this whole period, however, they scatter a thick, black carpet of seeds that appears to have a 100 percent germination rate. Each new plant puts down a taproot that grows like it thinks it's a tree. Daniel, the weeder, and I, the seeder, have differing opinions about Welsh poppy, but neither of us passes it on to those who request it without offering the same warning that we were given.

For me, individual plants, with their unique characteristics and idiosyncracies are the lifeblood of the garden. I marvel at their biological strengths and weaknesses as well as their beauty and scent. I shamelessly evaluate their acceptability based on how well suited they are to our needs as we develop and maintain this acre of hillside garden. Can they help us control the weeds? Can they reproduce themselves sufficiently to be visible in such a garden? Can they co-exist with the other plants we also love? What part of the year will they dominate a particular bed and how will that time dovetail with the demands of other plants? How well will they withstand the range of weather conditions they may face? There are many gorgeous plants in our garden with flowers that are paragons of form, scent, color, and beauty, but some of the plants dearest to my heart are those that are truly our gardening partners, doing their share of the work. ❁

# 6

## Where Gardens Come From

### *The Garden's Many Contributors*

ANN

6.1
*Sanguinaria canadensis*

THE STREISSGUTH GARDENS DIDN'T DEVELOP SOLELY AS THE result of our conscious effort, nor did they develop single-mindedly from a set of garden designs or even a preconceived plan. They evolved, as our lives have evolved, from interests going back to our childhood days, from being born into gardening families where husband and wife gardened together, and from many gardening mentors and friends who contributed to our garden through their books, through their shared interest, and through their plants.

Our parents, passionate and lifelong gardeners themselves, taught us to love and to nurture plants and to value gardens for family life. From our earliest days, we've watched our parents build gardens, watched them select and care for the plants they loved, and shared with them the fruits of their efforts: shade from a favorite tree on a too-hot day, a play area constructed by them for one us in the midst of a lovely garden, an apple or an apricot picked at the right moment from fruit trees growing knee-deep in flowers. We both remember a carefully mowed lawn that was the center of summer play and activity, an outside eating area where we watched the magic of night descend at the end of day and a flurry of activity that pro-

67

duced candles to turn our faces into caricatures of ourselves in the flickering light. We've watched with interest as our parents tended the fragile new forms of life they brought home to the family, and their sadness when a treasured plant died or was eaten by a mole or a slug. We remember the places in our childhood gardens where the family dog was buried, and the birds and turtles as well. We remember lilacs as tall as the second-story window, and falling asleep in spring with their scent drifting in on the night air. We remember the sweet, warm smell of newly cut grass, the mountains of fall leaves to jump into when your father turned away from raking.

Daniel's father grew tulips and irises, building little cages of wire for the tulip bulbs to keep the moles and squirrels away. His mother loved her pink bedding roses in symmetrical panels in her lawn, edged with a border of tea roses. They often got their plants (like bloodroot [*Sanguinaria canadensis*], fig. 6.1) from Mr. Hopkins, who made periodic visits to Monroe from his Kirkland nursery. Her perennial borders of multicolored phlox, yellow and brown helenium, and many others, kept the garden in color even in the heat of summer. She had a shady dell of exotic ferns ordered from a special nursery in Milwaukee, Oregon, and large drifts of early spring bulbs that she and her neighbor, Wilda Hamilton, gardened together in the strip of land between their two gardens. She had the same garden for seventy years and saw generations of plants come and go. In our Seattle garden, offspring of these same plants have made major contributions: snowdrops, creamy-white *Primula vulgaris*, our special double pink primulas, a lower dell filled with exotic ferns whose names are now forgotten but who faithfully unfurl their long arms late each spring reaching out for another season. Many of our woodland paths are lined with comfrey and pulmonaria (fig. 6.2) from her garden—cream, blue/pink, and sky blue, with dappled leaves or green, wonderful ground covers requiring no care at all. Our "rust garden" has omphalodes (*Omphalodes cappadocica*) (fig. 6.3), because Daniel recalls this tongue twister of a name from Aunty Clark's (Maud Gray Clark) next-door garden in Monroe.

My English mother, herself from generations of cottage gardeners, started extensive gardens from scratch three times in her life. She and my father tamed a large hillside garden in the Monterey Hills of South Pasadena: he built carefully placed brick stairs from the street below to the street above, with a phalanx of flat terraces branching off symmetrically. Together they planted apricots, peaches, and mediterranean plants.

6.2
*Pulmonaria*

6.3
*Omphalodes cappadocica*

6.4
*Zantedeschia aethiopica*,
Calla lily

6.5
*Anemone × hybrida*
'Honorine Jobert'

Calla lilies (fig. 6.4), from starts she got from Aunty Henry's Altadena garden sixty years ago, grew in her garden in southern Oregon and continue to grow in our garden in Seattle. Japanese anemones (fig. 6.5), four-o'clocks and assorted lilies and bulbs have migrated north to our garden in the course of frequent visits across a period of many years.

Daniel's parents' garden in Monroe was designed by Seattle landscape architect Otto Holmdahl in the late 1920s. He gave their garden a definitive form that has influenced Daniel throughout his career as a designer. John A. and Carol L. Grant helped refine and augment his parents' garden in the 1930s. Through this, Daniel learned of their book *Trees and Shrubs for Pacific Northwest Gardens*. Our copy is the 1943 edition; we continue to find it extraordinary in its completeness, accuracy, and judgments. The book was released in a revised and enlarged edition in 1990, with contributions by Marvin Black, Brian Mulligan, Joseph Witt, and Jean Witt.

Thanks to the literary interests of Daniel and his mother, we have assembled what is indeed a substantial collection of gardening books. These we enjoy greatly for their stimulating and lovely photographs and drawings, for their accounts of garden design and planning, and for the marvelous information they convey about plant varieties and culture. In Appendix 2, we have listed and described our most-used references and the works of our favorite garden writers.

Our long-time association with local nurseryman Ned Wells (the initial buildings at Wells Medina Nursery were designed by Daniel and his lifelong friend and architectural partner Gene Zema) has resulted in important contributions to our gardens, as well as to countless other gardens in the area, through his good advice and the availability of his fine nursery stock. The University of Washington Arboretum in Seattle has also been a continuing source of inspiration through the seasons, especially when our own gardens were smaller and less time consuming. A bike trip to the arboretum in spring would always leave us eager to return home to enlarge our own collections of magnolias, large rhododendrons, cherries, nyssas, and oxydendrum, to have more trees whose flowers would tower above us. As we searched for spring flowers, fall colors, and the earliest winter blossoms for our hillside garden, we spent the rainiest days of winter going through catalogues from Wayside Gardens, White Flower Farm, Park's Seeds, Thompson and Morgan, Van Bourgundian, and others of special collections.

My parents took up farming in southern Oregon relatively late in their lives. Although their main crops were from their fruit and nut trees, they also gained self-sufficiency and extra income from raising vegetables, which they sold to local fruit and vegetable vendors selling at roadside shelters called "stands." With the help of the Oregon State College Extension Service and its local extension agent, the city gardeners became serious farmers. Their skill and enjoyment in producing their own food has enriched our purpose as city gardeners in Seattle, and we have dedicated the most suitable part of our hillside garden to the raised beds of our vegetable garden. The idea of eating from the garden throughout the summer is a special passion of mine, which Daniel's and Ben's efforts in building and filling the raised beds have made a reality.

6.6
*Primula japonica* seedlings self-sowing uphill

6.7
*Helleborus orientalis*

6.8
*Trillium chloropetalum*
var. *giganteum*, black
trillium

Our gardens have also been influenced by our travel to other countries. The opportunity to visit estate and cottage gardens in England when we lived in Gloucestershire during our 1971–72 sabbatical year made a deep impression on us. On Sundays, we followed the schedule of the National Gardens Scheme (NGS) (though we knew the NGS as the Visiting Nurses' Sunday Garden Event), available widely in Great Britain, which listed several private gardens in close proximity—one of which would be serving tea and biscuits—open to the public on a specific Sunday. During the week we took trips to other important gardens we had read about. Our choices of many plants in our present gardens derive from those excursions. The robust *Clematis montana* clambering over the railings on the bridge to our oval lawn and up to frame the eastern upper door of our house (see fig. 2.8) was suggested by the vines at Great Dixter, Christopher Lloyd's house and garden in Sussex, where they covered old hop sheds with cascades of spring bloom and filled the air with their heady scent. Despite our efforts, we have failed repeatedly to replicate on our Schonacker garage roofs the dense clematis cover that we so admired on our 1972 visit to Great Dixter. Our black composition garage roofs must be too hot in summer for our

clematis to do as well as their British cousins do on Sussex tiles.

Our beech "tapestry hedge" forming the semicircular outdoor room above the Blaine Street stairs (see fig. 2.17) was suggested by the outdoor rooms we saw at Hidcote and other gardens, which were often enclosed by several varieties of a deciduous tree, such as hornbeam or beech, whose branches were intertwined to produce a virtual tapestry of leaf in the summer and a permeable woven basket of branches in winter. As our garden developed, we thought of the famous primula garden under the linden trees at V. Sackville-West's Sissinghurst and of Wisley Gardens outside London, where we first saw drifts of *Primula japonica* on the verges of streams. In our replication, they have self-sowed uphill along an old stream bed (fig. 6.6). The Exbury Gardens in Hampshire inspired us to plant in our own woods many of the Exbury azaleas developed there and to clear out several rather nice native elderberry clumps to provide sufficient spring sun. Our interest in *Rhododendron williamsianum* and some of its hybrids, such as 'Bowbells' and 'Moonstone', began after our visit to Bodnant in Wales. There, vast hillsides and ravines were planted in rhododendrons. Some of these plants had grown as large as garages.

Several years later, on a visit to Windsor Castle at Christmas we found

6.9
*Viola sororia*, confederate violet

*Viburnum × bodnantense* 'Dawn' in full bloom in below-freezing weather, planted in a protected area in what had once been a moat. Upon returning home, we were able to buy one from Ned Wells. We planted it in a low, protected place behind the old Schonacker garages, the first plant in what has now become our Winter Dell, filled with all manner of early flowering plants prospering in as much winter sun, and with as much wind protection, as we can provide. A fairly large *Daphne odora*, earlier languishing on our sandy and windy hillside above, is now thriving and blooming well in this protected spot. The hellebore from Daniel's mother's garden (fig. 6.7), happily seeding itself throughout the Dell, is living with black trillium (fig. 6.8) from Fred Rosenzweig, a lifelong Monroe friend who knew Daniel as a small boy; until his recent death, Fred still called him "Danny." Jack-in-the-pulpit bulbs (or, "horse and rider," as my Dutch horticulturist cousins call them) were a parting gift from those cousins on an earlier trip to Holland.

Many other relatives and dear friends have shared their favorite plants with us. Each year we eagerly await the return of their flowers in our garden, gentle reminders of the enduring friendships. Their gifts of plants have lived on in our garden long after the friends and relatives themselves are gone. "Did you see how Sylvia Epstein's confederate violets are spreading into the entry walk?" Daniel might announce happily on a warm spring day (fig. 6.9), or I might exclaim, "Agnes's naked ladies are out!" (fig. 6.10). It is impossible to walk through the gardens at any time of year without seeing the faces of the many old friends, and of their now-grown children, who have contributed to the gardens.

In the past few years, the garden has developed its own friends, and they too bring offerings of plants. Sometimes without a word, a nameless plant appears at our doorstep; we plant it and watch with interest to

6.10
*Amaryllis belladonna*,
naked ladies

6.11
*Iris ungicularis*

see what develops. Sometimes garden visitors bring us plants from their gardens that they know we've lost in ours or have been wanting. Our replacement *Iris unguicularis* (fig. 6.11) is the most notable example, but there are many others. We earlier had a veritable mass of this Algerian iris, the wonderful little blue that flowers earliest of all in December or January. Over the years we divided the clump for so many friends for so many other gardens that our own plant disappeared. Recently, upon hearing of our loss, a stair-runner gave us a vigorous new start. We have it in a place the books say it will love, as dry and sunny as we can provide, and, happily, it has already begun to bloom. Some plants have been brought by birds. The *Campanula medium* that now forms a semicircle of large sky-blue bells inside the bronze new growth on the tapestry hedge was initially bird-borne. Fortunately, it multiplied rapidly. A sweet pink perennial aster is another bird-delivered blessing.

A garden like ours is a complex compilation of items and ideas from many sources. Some of the most wondrous are the things we have given one another for the garden and through the garden. There's the sixty-fifth birthday *Magnolia campbellii* (see fig. 3.23), the fifty-fifth birthday *Rhododendron viscistylum* (see fig. 3.17), the Father's Day teak benches in the oval, the Valentine's Day 'Tilton' apricot, and the mizubachi (Japanese stone water basin) from our first Christmas together. There are constant little surprises and joys from gardening together as a family. The many things we have expressed to each other through the gardens are of central significance in the effects we see. The gardens reflect the totality of our lives and loves. ❁

# 7

## On Collections

*Our Special Interests Reflected in Our Gardens*

DANIEL

I N OUR GARDENING, AS IN OTHER REALMS OF OUR LIVES, WE OFTEN find ourselves entangled in contradictions. Our general garden conception is that we grow a great variety of the plants that we love and in which we find interest. We say that we don't specialize in huge collections of plants forming a mass of bloom in a specific season, or in plants of a single genus, species, or color, or of rare or relatively unknown varieties. We don't grow plants requiring highly specific growth conditions or plants too difficult or too tender in our climate. Nonetheless, we do find ourselves greatly enjoying a number of real collections of types and colorations of plants in some of the genera and species we most cherish. A few indeed are difficult and only marginally hardy, and a few do require very specific care and location, a few may be unusual.

Take our iris, for example. In the 1930s, my iris-fancying father and his gardening friends grew a number of the then-new bearded hybrids in pink, clear blue, and blackish-purple. There's apparently been a generational transmission of this interest, as our gardens seem to have lots of iris too (fig. 7.1). We have a host of beardeds, and around several of the boggy ponds we've

7.1
Tall bearded iris

introduced *Iris douglasiana*, the evergreen Pacific Coast native bearing white or mauve-blue flowers, and the tall-stemmed, yellow, moisture loving *I. forrestii*. Also in these moist soils, we grow the delicate violet-red *I. kaempferi*, plus a number of the kaempferi hybrids that the Japanese have developed into big, flat-flowered varieties. These are our latest-blooming irises, beginning in early June and continuing into July (fig. 7.2). Nearby, in drier soil, we grow Siberian iris (*I. sibirica*) in traditional blue and in white and some of the new sibirica-based hybrids. Elsewhere we grow *I. innominata*, the low-growing floriferous plant found and named relatively recently in southwestern Oregon, a white, a yellow, and a striped blue.

We have several *Iris tenax* and *I. missouriensis* from seed brought by a friend years ago, and, of course, *I. unguicularis* (fig. 7.3). We grow several Louisianas—slender-petaled copper-reds—and have several big beds of an evergreen we believe to be another *I. douglasiana*, which Ann collected on Mount Tamalpais a year before our marriage, this one, a clear, pale lavender-rose. The reticulatas, tiny bulb iris that flower in sharp blues and purples in February, don't persist for us longer than a year or two, but they are appealing enough for us to buy anew every few years to add again to the garden. We've had, but lose, from time to time, *I. graminea*, a tiny, violet-scented, almost ground-covering variety. We have vigorous leaves each year but ne'er a flower from a black species, *I. chrysographes*, and scarcely a flower either from our yellow *I. danfordiae* plants that bloom predictably the year following their planting but hardly ever again. *I. bucharica*, also yellow and white, on the other hand, does bloom predictably on the Rock Wall Path.

7.2
Japanese iris 'Peacock Dance'

7.3
*Iris unguicularis*

We find ourselves hosts to other collections as well, which together form a major part of our perennial gardens and provide some of our most rewarding and least difficult plantings. In the private garden sector, athwart a sunny shoulder between the oval lawn and the Blaine Street stairway, we grow a collection of midsummer blooming perennials—most desirable for us in extending the explosion of bloom in May and June into July and even August. These include monkshood, with its somber purple, blue and white cowls; *Filipendula rubra* 'Venusta', tall stems of pink, cloud-like blossoms swaying handsomely in breezes; and the four plants we can recall relatively easily because their names all begin with "l": lysimachia, lythrum, linaria, and liatris.

*Lysimachia clethroides* (see fig. 5.8) is for us most decorative and persistent, if invasive, and is fine for cutting in summer bouquets. Our variety of *Lythrum salicaria* is apparently different from the plant threatening to swamp many wetlands throughout the United States. Ours is a shy spreader, growing in tall spikes of magenta, its seed not vital. *Linaria purpurea*, with luminously silver-blue foliage and spikes of tiny flowerets of lavender or pink, is a vigorous self-seeding biennial or triennial. Ours is descended from seed that my father originally purchased at the Butchart

7.4
*Hemerocallis lilioasphode-lus*, lemon lily

Gardens in British Columbia in the 1930s and that continuously reseeded in the family garden (and later in ours), for nearly seventy years, occasionally throwing off a pink-flowered sport causing much excitement. *Liatris spicata* we like to group with the other "l" plants because it grows adjacent to them, though it blooms earlier than the others in the group. It has plumed, reddish-violet blossom heads, opening curiously from top to bottom of the plume instead of in the more usual bottom to top emergence.

We have a sizeable collection of daylilies. As do most gardeners, we find them admirably easy to grow and to divide, most rewarding in flower, drought resistant, and pest free. Many of ours have been purchased as named varieties over the years, and we have since lost their names, though we do remember 'Hyperion' and 'J. A. Crawford'. Our earliest bloomer is a short-stemmed clear yellow, each plant a mass of flowers in late May. Surely our favorite of all is the pale-yellow, gorgeously scented, old-fashioned lemon lily (fig. 7.4) from Ann's parents, but we have also a splendid range of hybrids in colors from coffee-brown through brownish-red to reddish-orange, bright yellow, yellowish-mauve, and on into some of the newer purple hybrids. We say we try not to be interested in faddish plants, but we admit to an interest in growing these purples and the new creamy near-whites (perhaps another contradiction on our parts, as we have habitually disdained hybridizers' tendencies to infuse the flowers of one variety with the characteristics of another—to develop peony-flowered tulips, white marigolds and white daylilies, and so forth). We prefer many of the traditional older varieties of daylilies, with their delicate star-shaped flowers, over most newer diploids and tetraploids with

7.5
Phlox!

7.6
*Astilbe × arendsii*
'Ostrich Plume'

7.7
The garden above Ann's
house

broader, heavier, form, though we are quixotically fascinated by the newer bi-colors with contrasting throats, or alternatingly colored petals, and we love greatly our peach tetraploid, a gift from South Carolina friends years ago. We've made recent additions to our daylily groups from our great gardening friend Kimberly Mills, who has an outstanding collection at her Bainbridge Island home. (She also grows spectacular collections of shrub roses, Austin hybrid roses, and others.) Kimberly's mother was an ardent amateur hybridizer, developing many fine new daylily varieties, of which we now have two ('Big Boy Bubba' and 'Coleman's Dream') of those she named.

Phlox! How much they contribute to our summer pleasure (fig. 7.5). Not quite as easy as daylilies, their foliage wilts if too dry. Our plants need deep hand-watering on hot summer days, when our sandy soil retains too little moisture, and some plants are mildew-prone if the foliage is drenched while watering, or if summer rains or humidity are excessive. But what glorious masses of flowers they give us, what clouds of powdery delicate fragrance. Most of our plants are starts from my mother's garden—phlox were probably her favorite of all plants. Many of the original plants were purchased from the old Ohio-based Wayside Gardens

7.8
*Aruncus dioicus*, goat's
beard

7.9
*Helenium autumnale*

and from a phlox nursery in Issaquah, its name now forgotten. Many of
the names are forgotten, too, save for 'Russian Violet', and the vigorous,
pure white 'Mt. Fuji'. The color range includes clear shell-pinks, pale
violets, purples, red-throated whites, with only a few plants in the coral-
pink or brassier orange-red ranges for contrast. The plants flower most
heavily if deadheaded during the summer, though we do not always take
the time to do it. The only other care they need, aside from summer
watering, is to pull the spent stalks in the late autumn and to apply a thick
mulch, a top dressing of manure and compost, in the late winter. We don't
dig this in, as the plants have heavy surface roots that dislike being disturbed. Phlox are easily divided, and it is a yearly joy to share divisions
with gardening friends. Our phlox bed, with stems cut to the ground in
winter, provides an ideal home for small spring-blossoming bulbs like
hyacinth, chionodoxa, jonquil, and snowdrop, all flowering and in leaf
before the later-developing phlox emerge.

Still another collection—this one color-based and season-based instead
of species-based—is the perennial group on the steep, moist hillside behind
Ann's house. Here in early summer are masses of the white, pink, and red
astilbes (fig. 7.6) that we described in chapter 2, flanked by white billows
of Shasta daisies (fig. 7.7), all backed by a towering clump of goat's beard
(fig. 7.8) as a creamy white terminus. Giving real piquancy to these assorted
whites, pinks, and reds, we grow clumps of vibrantly rust-colored helenium. Their semi-spherical brown seed mass matures first at the base of
the dome, erupting into fuzzy yellow stamens, the maturing then creeps
up the centers until at last the dome has changed from all brown to all

yellow (fig. 7.9). Along the border of the brick walk we grow the foot-high chartreuse-flowered *Euphorbia polychroma* as an additional color seasoning to the pinks and reds of the dominant astilbes.

We have struggled for years with another collector's item, and although many times we have tried seedlings and purchased starts, only in recent years have we had success: one vital specimen of *Franklinia alatamaha* (fig. 7.10), which is said to be the one and only species in this genus. The tree is described as having been found in the eighteenth century growing along the banks of the Alatamaha River in Georgia. It has been established in garden collections but has now become extinct in the wild. Ours seems to need both moisture and protection; it is now a wand about ten feet high, bearing attractive pointed leaves which color a lovely deep crimson maroon in autumn at the same time the buds open into winsome camellia-like white single flowers, centered with a boss of fuzzy yellow stamens. Our tree blooms shyly; in October 2003, it bore three flowers.

Still another collection item heightens the intensity of summer blossoming around the oval lawn, and stands in for the perennials bordering it when these plants are going over in late July and August. We use many potted annual plants and big pots of white and pink-flecked oriental lilies, of which 'Casa Blanca' is our favorite (fig. 7.11). These are heavily scented on the long, warm evenings of summer. One ten-inch pot of older bulbs had 76 five-inch blossoms this summer. Our yellow tiger lilies also grow in pots around the oval, all but the first grown from the little bulblets that appear above the leaf after the bloom fades. They are favorite gifts for garden visitors, easily replaced in three years' time. Our favorite annu-

7.10
*Franklinia alatamaha*

7.11
Potted lilies beside oval lawn, August

als for pots are old standby plants that bloom for many weeks, or even months: petunias, salpiglossis, cleome, lobelia, French marigold, nicotiana, heliotrope, and aquilegia. A fringe benefit in using potted annuals is that those in smaller pots can be used as centerpieces for outside dining. All the pots are of terra cotta (fig. 7.12), and they sit on the brick border surrounding our lawn. Each pot is filled with a rich mixture of compost and manure and is fed every two weeks with liquid fertilizer when watered.

We also use summer-blooming annuals to intermix with perennials on the hillside garden, especially above the Raccoon Pool, where they can co-exist with spring-blooming bulbs in a patch that catches good summer sun. Ann grows giant cactus-flowered zinnias (fig. 7.13) from seeds started indoors in May. We love the luscious, clear rose-red called 'Profusion Cherry', which we combine with giant single cosmos in shades of pink, red, and white. The cosmos seeds are saved yearly from our own plants. Delicate shirley poppies in the same hues and a tall, angular, lavender-colored *Verbena bonariensis*, which self-sows vigorously for us, were originally a gift from our neighbor, landscape architect Robert Chittock.

There are, of course, many additional collections. We've earlier described our group of scented rhododendrons, the Winter Dell and the shrub roses, the deciduous trees selected for autumn color to widen the coloration range of the hillside maples, the clumps of Exbury azalea, the groups of magnolia and stewartia. Our biggest collection is, of course, the food-producing group that includes all our vegetables, herbs, fruits, and berries. We understand that our garden, in its entirety, is itself a special collection of plants that compose themselves well on our hillside and thrive in our soils and climate. These plants hold meaning for us, are useful to us, and give us pleasure.

We have come to realize, indeed, that all the world's gardens are such special collections, and that if this is so, the word "garden" may be defined

7.12
Terra cotta pots with tiger lily seedlings, in winter

ON COLLECTIONS: OUR INTERESTS REFLECTED IN OUR GARDENS

7.13
Zinnia hybrids, with
cosmos

as a collection of elements and plants selected and combined by human hand. More generally, we realize that, in the same terms, many other man-made environments (like those we call farms or orchards or public parks) not usually called gardens are indeed gardens, too. Most generally, it seems that all the world's natural environments, though not touched by mankind, may also be called gardens; all are combinations, collections, of growing materials that have evolved in adaptation to landform, geology, climate: the Sonoran Desert, terraced Mediterranean hillsides, Amazon rain forests, and our own coniferous Pacific Coast forest, the Palouse wheat fields, the Cascade Mountain alpine meadows—all of these are gardens, as is ours. ✾

# 8

## Growing Up in the Garden and Getting Educated to Maintain It

BENJAMIN

MY EARLIEST MEMORIES OF "WORKING" IN THE GARDEN are from old photographs and family stories (fig. 8.1). A 1973 photograph of me picking up fragrant quinces (*Chaenomeles japonica* 'Snow Queen') by the front of the house suggests that I started working in the garden at age three. Like some plants that persist in your mind long after they disappear from the garden, this photo of me and the quince has gone missing. An extensive search turned up a related photograph (fig. 8.2), proving that the memory wasn't a figment of our imaginations. Other images linked to stories of my time in the garden show me carrying broken concrete (see fig. 3.2) and working on the Woodland Path (see fig. 1.16). Playing in the garden behind the house (now called the private garden) was a large part of my childhood, too, even though few specific memories or stories persist (figs. 8.3, 8.4, and 8.5).

My first actual memory of playing in the garden is of rolling croquet balls down clay trenches between the S-Steps and the Blaine Street stairs. Even at that early age, I think I understood what a challenge the nearly solid clay "soil" was going to pose for this garden, since every time I work in that bed today, I still think back to that time and realize how much the soil quality has improved since then.

Somewhere around this time, I started my morning "run" with the family dog along the path which at this time was the sole route across the

8.1
Ben and Daniel gathering leaves, 1973

8.2
Ben and Daniel gathering quinces

8.3
Ben and Katharine Scott playing dress-up

hillside. As I grew, so did the path system. Other strong childhood memories of the woods include my spending hours with the neighborhood girl, traipsing though the English ivy and collecting old beer bottles in large piles along the newly created Woodland Path (fig. 8.6). We wondered all the time why the people above felt they could use this lot as a garbage dump! It's a wonder neither of us ever got a serious cut from the glass we were handling. From collecting beer bottles, I graduated to pulling horsetails and eventually to removing blackberries. As I grew into a teenager I started mowing the grass, but somehow I never found that as interesting or rewarding as the more maintenance-oriented tasks, such as weeding, pruning, and clearing brush.

My first memories of doing garden tours with my parents are also from my early teenage years, though I'm sure I was present on many earlier garden tours. I never remember actively learning flower names as I was growing up, and I was surprised as a young adult at how many I had picked up. Around age sixteen, I got my first job outside the garden, at a neighbor's house, transplanting rhododendrons and weeding her hillside. I worked there off and on for two years until I went away to university.

The last two years of high school were particularly exciting because of the effort to protect the three lots south of our garden from further development by nominating them for preservation of open space status by the city parks department. Those three lots had been less than pristine my entire life. I strongly remember the shock of coming home one day from second grade to find heavy machinery clearing a road up though the lots. I remember crying, feeling so upset at the possible loss of these woods to more building, and hoping that the greenbelt at the end of the street would still have some access point so I could go and play in it. How long the work on these lots lasted I don't remember, but I'm sure it wasn't more

8.4
Ben at play on the deck

8.5
A typical day with friends in the sand pile

GROWING UP IN THE GARDEN

than a couple of months. We were left with a flat, level road across the east side of those three lots, and that road became the principal access to the greenbelt. In the 1990s (at the time of the nomination), the lots were still a little raw. They continued to show signs of the heavy machinery that had been literally dragged through the site, and several of the large slash piles had not fully settled (fig. 8.7). The prospect of saving those lots for future greenbelt space was particularly appealing because the natural revegetation process had already started. All three of us eagerly attended as many of the parks department meetings as possible, hoping finally to see those lots covered with trees again.

That fall, I went off to study computer science back east. Among the highlights I was eager for that fall were letters from home with updates on the progress of the green spaces nomination. I remember being caught at least once for reading a letter from home in class when I should have been listening to the professor. During the five-week winter break that year, I returned home and my dad and I built the retaining wall down at the street and the raised vegetable beds (see fig. 3.5). This is probably the single largest project undertaken in the garden during my life. I remember fondly being out there in the rain, cutting blocks of solid blue clay as if they were slabs of butter and marveling at the difference between the clay in winter and in summer.

After my first year at the eastern university, I returned home in May. That summer could be considered the start of my career in landscaping, as I took on several weeding and pruning projects around the neighborhood, in addition to building more raised vegetable beds at my best friend's parents' summer home. The nomination of the land to be purchased for greenbelt was slowly churning its way through the process of public meetings and review boards as the city considered which parcels they would

8.6
Constructing the Woodland Path, 1976

8.7
View of skid road, twenty years after being cleared; new clearing begins, to start garden expansion

purchase. The following Christmas I dropped out of the university in favor of studying computer programming at a community college in Seattle. As summer returned, I added a couple of clients to my project list. Since I was still living at home, I resumed working in the ever expanding garden, tending, as boys do, to favor the more strenuous tasks and often opting to carry large armfuls of brush instead of weeding.

I'm not sure when the idea of sharing the garden with the general public started, but I think I first became aware of this concept as I was working more and more in the garden. There is a wonderful energy in the garden derived from having other people wander though it or admire it from its boundaries, and I took it upon myself to encourage even more people to use and enjoy the garden.

The garden may have been a more forceful influence on me than I recognized, because the following summer, 1992, I again quit school. This time I was looking for temporary work until I discovered what career path I wanted to follow. I had spent my entire life playing with computers, and suddenly I knew there was little future in it for me. My experience in gardening and plants led me to a job selling plants at a nursery. I don't think it hurt that the woman who hired me knew our garden and had enjoyed walking through it when she had lived close by a few years earlier. I was convinced that I knew little about plant names when I started work but was quickly proven wrong. Much to my surprise, I often knew a greater number of plant names than did the other teenagers who had been working at the nursery for several summers. This familiarity with plants, plus my experience in gardening, helped me when later that summer I officially opened my own landscaping business, with the help of clients from the nursery who were looking for landscapers. The only down side to working in the landscaping business was that it no longer seemed fun to work with my parents in our garden. I tended to drift away from our garden and was less excited than I should have been when the garden and the other three lots became part of the St. Mark's greenbelt (fig. 8.8).

Seven years after starting my business, and still very much absorbed in it, I discovered that my temporary job was turning into a career. However, I felt that to succeed more fully, I needed more schooling. In the spring of 1999, I began studying horticulture at Edmonds Community

8.8
Ben and Daniel checking out the greenbelt

GROWING UP IN THE GARDEN

College. Within weeks of starting school, I found myself excited again about our garden and its potential. I used the garden for as many projects as I could, and I tried to rally some of my favorite teachers into using our garden as a teaching tool. I was not able to do as much work in the garden as I would have liked during the first few years of school, so I sought to contribute in other ways. It became clear to me that if this garden were to become a successful *public* garden, it would need a greater following of people than the several hundred who knew about it.

During a class on Public Garden Management, I hatched my first major project: a plant tagging system. The engraved black plastic tags that we eventually chose are loosely modeled after those in the Washington Park Arboretum. They list both the full botanical name (genus and species) and the common name (fig. 8.9). Many of the woody plants in the garden are now labeled so people can easily identify them. We've chosen not to label every individual plant, but have tried to label the most conspicuous specimen of each plant. When we started, we had an out-of-date and incomplete base map of the garden. While I researched and experimented with plant tags, my dad completed the drawing that located most of the woody plants and a few special herbaceous plants. This garden plan provided the history of some of the plants and also made it clear that we needed an easy way to locate duplicate plants (for instance, there are now eighteen 'PJM' rhododendrons in the garden, but only one is tagged). I knew that a database would be the easiest way to track this information and archive the garden's history.

Building on our desire to increase public awareness of the garden and to increase the garden's potential as a tool for learning, my next project was to set up a Web site that would not only tell the history of the garden but could also be used by people seeking information from the database. A number of years earlier I had done a small Web site in what was then the fledgling World Wide Web. The old site had disappeared less than a year after it was born, and I wanted to make sure that the new one would stick around for a long time. The wealth of information in the database, I felt, should be incorporated into the Web site in addition to basic particulars about the plants. In the course of developing the site, I decided to add photographs of each plant for cataloging and identification purposes. Thus was born my third project: to take photos of most of the plants in the garden and, additionally, to try to highlight some of the seasonal

8.9
Typical plastic plant tag in The Streissguth Gardens

Laurus nobilis
Bay Laurel

interests. It took nearly two years of data entry and Web programming (as well as tackling other issues, such as setting up a LAN and a Web server that was fairly secure, installing DSL, and purchasing our own domain) before the Web page premiered (fig. 8.10) . It came online just in time for a three-quarter-page article on the Streissguth Gardens in one of the local daily newspapers (see the Web site for a link). The creation of the site became one of several key elements in my application for admission to the University of Washington's Department of Landscape Architecture.

During my four years at community college, our garden had become an increasingly important part of my life. About halfway through my education, it dawned on me that I was extremely interested in continuing to maintain the garden after my parents were no longer able to care for it. Again, I wanted to return to the garden, and I started trying to spend a day a week (or so) working there. It also led to the realization that I didn't want to run a maintenance business because I no longer found it fun to work in our garden after spending forty hours working in other people's gardens. Around this same time, I came to understand that I was less interested in specific cultivars of plants and was searching for more design theory.

With a little nudge from a guest lecturer in one of my classes and from a friend who was taking a class in landscape architecture, I explored the department at the University of Washington. I took one class that spring and knew then that I wanted to apply as soon as I could (which turned out to be in about a year). That summer I took a beginning design studio and was completely hooked on the department. I had finally found a group of people who were interested in plants, architecture, the environment, and city planning. While applying to that department, I became aware that over the years, I had developed an interest in the system of greenbelts that runs though Seattle—and interested in the way the public uses it.

I was accepted into the UW Bachelor of Landscape Architecture program and started school in the fall of 2003. Following in the personal tradition I had started at Edmonds Community College, I have used the gardens (and the surrounding greenbelt) as my focus for several projects, most notably for a database of native woody plants found between Puget Sound and the 3,000–foot elevation mark in the Cascades. The information from this database is now on the Web site. I hope to integrate this information into future projects in the gardens.

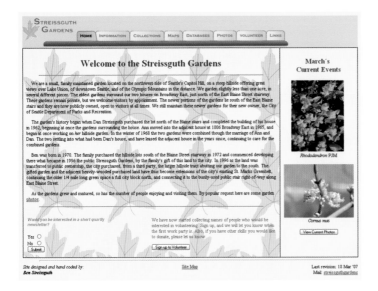

8.10
The Streissguth Gardens Web site

After completing my first year in the landscape architecture program, I headed to Rome to study for three months; the program sends a group of students every other year to study there. I welcomed the chance for a brief change of environment, a change in focus, as well as a different (though in no way less vigorous) pace of life. This shift came at an opportune time, as I was still figuring out the right niche for myself in the general field of landscape architecture. The field is broad enough, however, that I stand a good chance of successfully melding my interests in horticulture, public garden management, greenbelts, and parks.

I completed my degree at the university and took a six-month temporary position in the University of Washington's irrigation department. During this time, many evenings were spent designing an irrigation system for our garden. I am now working with the Seattle Parks Department to obtain a dedicated water meter and permission to install the system I have designed. After my irrigation work at the university, I joined a landscape architecture firm. I am thrilled finally to have a career I enjoy and still have time and energy to devote to the garden.

My next plan for providing educational opportunities within the garden is to create a display garden of native plants. This area would serve as a transition between our garden and a partly restored section of the greenbelt. The far edge of the restored greenbelt would merge into the unmanaged greenbelt just to the south of the three lots the City of Seattle purchased. I feel that this is an important link to the garden because it shows the full range of possibilities for gardening within the city and recalls that our garden started with nothing more than the wilds of the unmanaged greenbelt. ❀

# 9

## Looking Back, Looking Ahead

DANIEL, ANN, AND BENJAMIN

W E STREISSGUTHS ARE INDEED "IN LOVE WITH A HILLSIDE garden"! Why do we love it? How has gardening in the city, and giving a garden to the city, benefited our lives? What have we learned worthy of being passed on to other citizen-gardeners? Our answers are complex and diverse. Here they are for this point in our lives:

❋ Our house and gardens have given us transcendent joy during forty years. We've reveled in sights and aromas, in the excitement of plant growth and maturity, in the pleasure of planning and toil, and in the satisfaction of reaping the outcomes of our efforts. The physical challenges of bending, crawling, climbing, and carrying contribute to our continuing good health, as do our exposure to sunshine, clean air, and fresh vegetables and fruits.

❋ Our gardens have become a powerful focus of family interest and activity and have knit the three of us solidly together in a way that our other individual bents have never done. We use the gardens continually for outdoor dining (figs. 9.1 and 9.2), outdoor living, and family recreation (fig. 9.3).

❋ The configuration of our house and gardens derives, of course, from our own persons, but it comes importantly as well from the relationship

9.1
Dinner, with hats and
friends the Neffs, on
the oval, 1991

9.2
Ann and bride-to-be
Ruth Little; luncheon
on the oval, 1997

9.3
Exercising new puppy,
Tiger, 1998

of our land to surrounding landforms, community, and public walks and streets. Our immediate outlooks and our views of the larger city and region stimulate us every day. Through the gardens, we establish links with a wide variety of people we would otherwise never encounter. Some are neighbors who use "our" public stairway to and from their residences, schools, metro stops, and work places. Some are strangers who stumble upon the garden unexpectedly trying to get up or down Capitol Hill. Some come from across the greater Seattle area to use the stairs for exercise and workouts (figs. 9.4 and 9.5). For this group, weekends are the busiest, sometimes with several hundred runners and walkers. Others come especially to see the gardens (fig. 9.6), either coming regularly to enjoy the constant change, or at special seasons to see favorite plants in bloom. Some come with relatives or friends to share what one family

9.4
Runner on Blaine
Street landing

9.5
Runners on Blaine
Street stairs flanked by
*Rhododendron* 'Azor'

called "a little piece of paradise in the city." We easily become acquainted with many of these passers-by and visitors. Some become good friends with whom we share ideas on life. Some of the garden enthusiasts become gardening buddies with whom we share plants and garden tours. These human contacts generated by our busy stairway include people of many ages, backgrounds, and persuasions. We know that we are stronger for the diversity of these personal links. We know that the widening of our horizons helps to counteract the tendency of lives, in aging, to narrow and become more isolated from society.

❀ Our 1996 gift of the garden to the City of Seattle was motivated principally by our resolve to share our garden riches with the public, by our hope to ensure the gardens' long-term future, and by our deeply felt wish to make a significant contribution to the city we love so much. The gift has changed and benefited our lives in many ways, though we did not fully understand all of these at the time of the transfer. We had known that there would be some effect on our family income-tax obligations, but as we prepared our forms in 1997, our accountant, needing to know the dollar value of our gift, asked for a professional real estate appraisal. We duly commissioned one, at some substantial cost, and were surprised at the estimates. As the land's value far exceeded our annual income, the accountant was able to prorate the amount over a five-year period, giving us, in each of the following five years, a big tax deduction (each year, one fifth the value of our gift). What a surprise! What a windfall! What to do with the unexpected asset in each of the next years? We knew at once: the tax savings would permit us to increase substantially our annual gifts to our usual beneficiaries (educational institutions, social services, arts and performing arts agencies, political candidates and causes, etc.). We describe all of this now in the hope that it may encourage others to consider making gifts, and increasing gifts, to communities, institutions, organizations—to the nation. We found that the gift of our garden to the city actually had a doubled effect: the value of the gift itself, plus the gift's ability to make a gift of the tax benefits.

❃ Another benefit of the garden is that it has helped us clarify what we really believe in. Had we been asked decades ago to state the principles underlying and directing the form of our house and the creation of our gardens, we're not sure we'd have been able to respond clearly. One of the great benefits of our years of living and gardening together is that we are now more certain of our principles, and not so reticent to share them in the pages of a book. Those principles are stated in our Introduction and are illustrated through the succeeding chapters. We state our beliefs about the relationship between a garden and its surrounding physical environment and that between a dwelling and a garden. We are sure that a garden must grow and change over time, that a garden requires its users' continuous commitment, that it be composed only of elements with meaning

9.6
The garden attracts strollers

9.7
The house reaches out to its community

to the gardeners. Finally, we describe a necessary beautiful link between house and garden and a surrounding community and the need for a nourishing interchange between the two (fig. 9.7).

❋ Our garden has had a satisfying, and we think worthy, educational impact on our community during its more than forty years. Visitors return again and again, neighborhood groups visit and use the gardens (fig. 9.8), and students of Daniel's who have worked here as gardeners now actively garden their own plots. Children from the nearby Bertschi School visit regularly to study and sketch plant life and to release butterflies they've raised in science classes (figs. 9.9 and 9.10). Children from the Brightwater School's third grade have helped to haul gravel for paths and to weed, cultivate, and clip back ivy. Children of our friends and neighbors have run on the magical pathways in a neighborhood Easter egg hunt which enchants children each year (fig. 9.11). Some of these same children return years later on their own. Some surely become a next generation of convinced gardeners.

❋ We anticipate that all these benefits, accrued over all these years, will keep accumulating in the twenty-first century. In the years ahead, we expect to continue as we're doing for as long as we are able, but there *are* new developments. We are undertaking new projects and challenges in the garden. We hope, we expect, that these will yield their own new group of garden accomplishments—to be added to subsequent lists.

Benjamin, in chapter 8, wrote of his establishing a Streissguth Garden Web site, with images of about 300 plant specimens and 900 entries in the database representing about 1,000 plants. He has described, too, his plant-tagging project, the initial concept a surprise Christmas gift one rainy Seattle winter. Ben and Daniel together have completed a 1/8–inch scale garden map, which has now become five feet long. This has been a major undertaking; while it is difficult to keep up to date, it is very useful in evaluating progress and change.

Currently, our most intensive work in the public garden is concentrated along its south edge, where the garden abuts the sector purchased by the city in 1996. We are aggressively planting there now, using many starts and divisions of favorite plants from our older gardens. We're interplanting domesticated varieties (poppies, lilies, geranium, astilbe) with many natives (sword fern, vine maple, vancouveria, garrya, salal, trillium, Pacific Coast iris) toward the goal of softening the transition between the established gardens and the wilder adjacent greenbelt, and toward Ben's goal of a native-plant display garden.

Our contract with the City of Seattle, at the time of our land gift, gives Dan and Ann, and Benjamin after us, the right and responsibility to continue to care for the garden. We hope that Ben will be able to do this, although he now lives away from us and from the garden, in his own house in the Central District; we know his life and obligations may change. We are currently training volunteers for Streissguth Gardens to help in the upkeep, and we hope that future generations of children will continue to enjoy and learn from the garden (fig. 9.12).

9.9
Caged butterflies ready
to release, June 2003

9.10
Free in the garden

We understand the need to plan how best to assure the future educational and pleasurable impact of the garden and to structure a long-term financial basis for its future care and development. We accept that responsibility and, in December 2007, have established a Streissguth Garden Foundation within the larger Seattle Parks Foundation, in the expectation that the endowment will continue to grow, ensuring the garden's care as a resource for all of the city in all the years ahead. ❀

9.11
Hunting Easter eggs in the garden

9.12
Bertschi kindergarten class doing a garden tour

# Appendix 1

## *Useful and Indispensable Tools*

THIS LIST INCLUDES MANY OF THE TOOLS WE USE DURING A TYPICAL garden year. The most indispensable ones (those we would have the hardest time gardening without) are marked with an asterisk:

* A good hand trowel,* a hand fork,* and a hori-hori*

* Hand pruning clipper,* grass shears,* garden scissors,* long-handled brush clipper, hedge shears (blades about a foot long), plus file* for sharpening all of the above

* A slender, folding brush saw (cutting on the pull stroke)

* A long-handled, extension, combination tree pruner and brush saw

* Several shovels,* long and short handled

* Metal rake, metal hoe

* Sturdy, generously sized gloves*: horsehide, canvas, goatskin for small jobs

* Bamboo plant stakes 3' long, cedar stakes 4' long

* Big roll of sisal garden twine*

❊ Baskets* (We like broad-based, lightweight "bushel" baskets.)

❊ Bamboo rakes* (For elasticity and cleaning efficiency, we find bamboo rakes superior to any metal grass/leaf rakes, though the tines do wear and the rakes need to be replaced annually.)

❊ Four-gallon sprayer fitted so it can be pumped while in use, strapped to the gardener's back

❊ Two-quart hand sprayer

❊ Knee or kneeling pads*

❊ Wheelbarrow

❊ Reel lawn mower plus grass catcher (Power movers are too noisy for us and too heavy to tote up and down stairs from their storage places.)

❊ Metal extension ladder or step ladder

❊ Axe and hatchet

❊ White plastic plant tags and wax pencils or indelible ink pens

❊ Terra cotta flower pots (We prefer these pots for their subtle colorations and individuality in aging despite their weight, their fragility, and their high moisture transmission. As we ourselves age, however, we are recognizing the virtues of plastic, which escaped us in our youth. Now Ann understands why her mother, at ninety, used those funky plastic pots on her terrace!)

# Appendix 2

*Useful Books in the Streissguths' Library*

OUR COLLECTION OF GARDEN BOOKS NUMBERS AT LEAST 150. MANY of these are general references; others are more specialized; some are simply inspiring and delightful in their literary or visual content. Some of our most indispensable, frequently used, and well-worn titles are recent. A number are old editions, and many of these may now be out of print. We list them here to suggest the range of garden writing for gardeners beginning their libraries and also to suggest the importance of supplementing real dirt-gardening experiences with guidance and inspiration from books.

## General Guides and References

Beales, Peter. *Classic Roses: An Illustrated Encyclopedia and Grower's Manual of Old Roses, Shrub Roses, and Climbers.* Austin, Tex.: Holt, Rinehart, and Winston, 1985.
*This beautifully illustrated volume is a trusted source of information on old and shrub roses. A revised and expanded edition is published by Henry Holt and Company, 1997.*

Graf, Alfred Byrd. *Exotica 2: Pictorial Cyclopedia of Indoor Plants.* Rutherford, N.J.: Roehrs Company, 1959.
*This hefty classic is a constant companion in our care and understanding of houseplants.*

Grant, John A., and Carol L. Grant. *Trees and Shrubs for Pacific Northwest Gardens.* Seattle: Published by F. McCaffrey for Dogwood Press, 1943.
*Of all our gardening books, this one has had the strongest influence on planting our Seattle garden. It is available in a revised edition (Timber Press, 1990), with added notes by Marvin Black, Brian Mulligan, Joseph Witt, and Jean Witt.*

Hay, Roy, and Patrick M. Synge. *The Color Dictionary of Flowers and Plants for Home and Garden.* Published in collaboration with the Royal Horticultural Society. New York: Crown Publishers, 1969.
*We use this regularly and consider it, or a comparable volume, mandatory in a garden collection.*

Kruckeberg, Arthur R. *Gardening with Native Plants of the Pacific Northwest: An Illustrated Guide.* Seattle: University of Washington Press, 1989.
*Dr. Kruckeberg's book on native plants is an unsurpassed Northwest gardener's aid.*

Leach, David G. *Rhododendrons of the World.* New York: Scribner Book Company, 1961.
*An essential book for its coverage of species and hybrids, culture and maintenance.*

*New Sunset Western Garden Book.* Rev. ed. Menlo Park, Calif.: Sunset Publishing Company, 2001.
*This book is an absolute necessity, constantly in use and of the greatest value.*

Phillips, Roger, and Martyn Rix. *Shrubs.* New York: Random House, 1989.

———. *Perennials.* Vol. 1: *Early Perennials.* New York: Random House, 1991.

———. *Perennials.* Vol. 2: *Late Perennials.* New York: Random House, 1991.

Thomas, Graham Stuart. *Perennial Garden Plants, or, the Modern Florilegium.* Portland, Ore.: Sagapress/Timber Press, 1990.
*We find this the most comprehensive of all the perennial plant guides.*

## Some Favorite Pictorial Books

Dillon, Helen. *Garden Artistry: Secrets of Designing and Planting a Small Garden.* New York: Macmillan Publishing Company, 1995.
*Dillon and Schinz (listed below) incorporate lovely photographic and written descriptions of, respectively, an Irish and an Italian garden. These two have been of great and specific inspiration to us in the preparation of our book.*

Hyams, Edward, and Edwin Smith. *The English Garden.* New York: Harry N. Abrams (n.d.) c. 1960s.
*There are several versions of this classic. Our heavy, undated edition measures 11 × 13 × 2 inches. It pictures all the best-known gardens of the British Isles.*

Schinz, Marina. *A Tuscan Paradise.* New York: Stewart, Tabori & Chang, 1998.

## Classics by British Gardeners

Jekyll, Gertrude. *Annuals and Perennials; Colour Schemes for the Flower Garden*;
and *Wall and Water Gardens*. London: Country Life Library.
*We are fortunate to have early editions of these three undated Jekylls. Others in her
series describe the design and construction of the Jekyll house and garden at Mun-
stead Wood. Many are available now in reprint editions.*

Lloyd, Christopher. *The Well-Tempered Garden*. London: Collins, 1971.
*This is one of many by or about this imaginative, opinionated, savvy superstar and
his Great Dixter garden.*

Nichols, Beverly. *Sunlight on the Lawn*. New York: E. P. Dutton and Company,
1956; *Garden Open Tomorrow*. London: Heinemann, 1968; *The Gift of a Garden*. New York: Dodd, Mead and Company, 1974.
*We have these three old editions of books Daniel's parents read in his childhood. He
shared their enjoyment then, as we do now. Many of the Nichols titles are available
in reprint editions.*

Sackville-West, Vita. *A Joy of Gardening*. New York: Harper and Row, 1958; *Vita
Sackville-West's Garden Book*. New York: Atheneum, 1968.
*These are two of many by (and about) this gardener and her husband and their gar-
den at Sissinghurst. All are instructive, exciting visually and intellectually.*

Verey, Rosemary. *The Garden in Winter*. Boston and Toronto: Little, Brown and
Company, 1988.
*This is the favorite of all the splendid books of hers in our collection. Each is inspir-
ing; all profit from her unerring eye and descriptive skills.*

## Garden Writing for Reading Pleasure

Goodman, Richard. *French Dirt: The Story of a Garden in the South of France*.
New York: Algonquin Books of Chapel Hill, 1991.
*An enchanting account by an American learning to garden in France.*

Page, Russell. *Education of a Gardener: A Personal and Somewhat Autobiographical
Treasury of Gardening by One of the World's Greatest Gardeners*. London and
Glasgow: Atheneum, 1962.
*The subtitle says it all.*

White, Katharine S. *Onward and Upward in the Garden* . New York: Farrar,
Straus, Giroux, 1979.
*One of many Katharine White titles, this anthology of garden articles done for The
New Yorker includes her renowned March 1958 review of gardening catalogues as
literature.*

Ben's Recommendations for Plant Identification and Detailed Information on Specific Plants and Their Maintenance

Baumgardt, John. *How to Identify Flowering Plant Families: A Practical Guide for Horticulturists and Plant Lovers.* Portland, Ore.: Timber Press, 1982.

Dirr, Michael A. *Manual of Woody Landscape Plants.* Champaign, Ill.: Stipes Publishing, 1998.
*While this book is oriented toward the East Coast, it contains the most in-depth information on woody plants of any of our references.*

DiSabato-Aust. *The Well-Tended Perennial Garden.* Portland, Ore.: Timber Press, 1998.

Hill, Susan, and Susan Marizny. *The Plant Locator Western Region.* Portland, Ore.: Timber Press, 2004; Cambridge, Mass.: Black-Eyed Susans Press, 2004.

Joyce, David, and Christopher Brickell. *American Horticultural Society Pruning and Training.* London and New York: D K Publishing, 1996.

Lord, Tony, principal ed. *RHS Plant Finder 2000–2001.* London: Dorling Kindersley Ltd., 2000.

Other General References We Used in Preparing This Book

Fiorella, Ann
*This former Eastlake/Capitol Hill resident assembled a private collection of historical materials documenting the history of the Capitol Hill public stairways, drawing from records of the Seattle Engineering Department, the Seattle municipal archives, the Museum of History and Industry, the University of Washington libraries, and other sources.*

Kruckeberg, Arthur R. *The Natural History of Puget Sound Country.* Seattle: University of Washington Press, 1989.
*Indispensable as a guide to understanding our soils, climates, landforms, etc.*

Williams, Jacqueline B. *The Hill with a Future: Seattle's Capitol Hill, 1900–1946.* Seattle: CPK Ink, 2001. ❋

# Appendix 3

*Plants Discussed in the Book, by Botanical/Common*
*and Common/Botanical Names*

THROUGHOUT THE TEXT, WE USE PLANT NAMES AS WE SPEAK OF them regularly, sometimes using botanical names or names of cultivars, sometimes using common names. Two plant lists follow: the first alphabetizes the botanical names; the second list alphabetizes the common names.

The plants in these two lists are gathered from specific references to individual plants throughout the text and are offered as an aid to the difficult task of matching common and botanical names. Botanical names of ornamental plants are based on information in *The RHS Plant Finder 2000–2001*; *The Pacific Northwest Plant Locator 1999–2000*; and *Manual of Woody Landscape Plants* (Michael Dirr, 1998). However, there remains disagreement among the family as to the "most correct" name. In some cases, we have chosen to stay with older names, despite knowing that they may be out of date. Weed names are from *Weeds of the West* (2000). For common names, we have chosen to follow the popular, though botanically incorrect, form of referring to cultivars in their common form with their apostrophes. We regret any confusion this may cause.

For additional plant information and characteristics, please see our Web site at http://www.streissguthgardens.com. In our database, we track standard characteristics (plant type, flower time, flower color, etc.), seasonal interest, specific collections, and location (both on a grid and by bed name). We have also provided multiple ways to search for plants, including by genus, by common name, by garden location, and by some of the other attributes (flower time, flower color, etc.). We hope this information will prove useful and will increase your pleasure in getting to know our garden and the plants within.

## Plants listed by Botanical Name

| Botanical Name | Common Name |
|---|---|
| *Acer circinatum* | Vine maple |
| *Acer macrophyllum* | Big leaf maple |
| *Aconitum napellus* | Monkshood |
| *Allium cepa* | Red onion |
| *Allium cepa* var. *viviparum* | Egyptian onion, walking onion |
| *Allium cepa* 'Walla Walla Sweet' | 'Walla Walla Sweet' onion |
| *Allium oschaninii* | Shallot |
| *Allium schoenoprasum* | Chives |
| *Amaryllis belladonna* | Naked ladies |
| *Anemone blanda* | Wind flower |
| *Anemone* 'Flore Pleno' | Double white anemone |
| *Anemone nemorosa* | Wood anemone |
| *Anemone × hybrida* 'Honorine Jobert' | Japanese anemone |
| *Anethum graveolens* | Dill |
| *Aquilegia* hybrids | Aquilegia, columbine |
| *Arabis caucasica* | Arabis |
| *Arctostaphylos columbiana* | Manzanita, hairy |
| *Arctostaphylos hookeri* | Monterey manzanita |
| *Arctostaphylos uva-ursi* | Kinnikinnick |
| *Arisaema triphyllum* | Jack-in-the-pulpit, horse and rider |
| *Aruncus dioicus* | Goat's beard |
| *Aster novae-angliae* | Pink aster |
| *Astilbe* 'Fanal' | 'Fanal' astilbe |
| *Astilbe × arendsii* 'Ostrich Plume' | 'Ostrich Plume' astilbe |
| *Astilbe × arendsii* 'Bridal Veil' | 'Bridal Veil' astilbe |
| *Aubrieta deltoidea* | Aubrieta |
| *Beta vulgaris* 'Detroit Dark Red' | 'Detroit Dark Red' beet |
| *Beta vulgaris* 'Fordhook Giant' | 'Fordhook Giant' Swiss chard |
| *Beta vulgaris* 'Vulcan' | 'Vulcan' Swiss chard |
| *Brassica napus* | Rape |
| *Caltha palustris* | Marsh marigold |
| *Calystegia sepium* | Morning glory |
| *Camassia cusickii* | Camass |
| *Camassia quamash* | Camass |
| *Camellia japonica* | Japanese camellia |
| *Camellia japonica* 'Finlandia' | 'Finlandia' camellia |
| *Camellia japonica* 'Howard Asper' | 'Howard Asper' camellia |
| *Camellia sasanqua* | Sasanqua camellia |
| *Camellia sasanqua* 'Briar Rose' | 'Briar Rose' camellia |
| *Camellia sasanqua* 'Vericolor' | 'Vericolor' camellia |
| *Campanula medium* | Campanula, Canterbury bells |
| *Campanula rotundifolia* | Dwarf campanula, harebells |
| *Capsicum annuum* 'Hungarian Red' | 'Hungarian Red' pepper |
| *Capsicum annuum* 'Hungarian Yellow' | 'Hungarian Yellow' pepper |
| *Carpenteria californica* | Carpenteria |
| *Chaenomeles speciosa* 'Nivalis' | 'Nivalis' flowering quince |
| *Chaenomeles japonica* 'Snow Queen' | 'Snow Queen' flowering quince |
| *Chelidonium majus* | Greater celandine |
| *Chimonanthus praecox* | Wintersweet |
| *Chionodoxa luciliae* | Chionodoxa |
| *Chrysanthemum maximum* | Shasta daisy |
| *Chrysanthemum parthenium* | Feverfew |
| *Cichorium endivia* | Endive, curly |
| *Cirsium arvense* | Thistle |
| *Cistus × hybridus* | White rockrose |
| *Clematis montana* | Montana clematis |
| *Clematis vitalba* | Wild clematis |
| *Cleome hasslerana* | Cleome, spider flower |
| *Consolida ajacis* | Larkspur |
| *Convallaria majalis* | Lily-of-the-valley |
| *Coptis trifolia* | Coptis, golden thread |
| *Cornus* 'Eddie's White Wonder' | 'Eddie's White Wonder' dogwood |
| *Cornus florida* | Eastern dogwood |
| *Cornus mas* | Cornelian cherry |
| *Cornus nuttallii* | Western dogwood |
| *Cornus stolonifera* | Redtwig dogwood |
| *Corylopsis pauciflora* | Buttercup winter hazel |
| *Corylopsis spicata* | Spike winter hazel |
| *Cosmos bipinnatus* | Cosmos |
| *Crataegus phaenopyrum* | Washington thorn |
| *Crocus tomasinianus* | Tomasinianus crocus |
| *Cucumis sativus* | Cucumber |
| *Cucurbita pepo* | Zucchini |

| | | | |
|---|---|---|---|
| *Cupressus sempervirens* 'Stricta' | Italian cypress | *Helenium autumnale* | Helenium |
| *Cyclamen coum* | Cyclamen | *Helianthemum nummularium* | Sunrose |
| *Cyclamen hederifolium* | Cyclamen | *Helianthemum* 'Wisley Pink' | 'Wisley Pink' sunrose |
| *Daphne odora* | Winter daphne | *Heliotropium arborescens* | Heliotrope |
| *Dianthus caryophyllus* | Carnation | *Helleborus orientalis* | Lenten rose |
| *Dianthus deltoides* | Maiden pink | *Hemerocallis* 'Big Boy Bubba' | 'Big Boy Bubba' daylily |
| *Digitalis purpurea* | Foxglove | *Hemerocallis* 'Coleman's Dream' | 'Coleman's Dream' daylily |
| *Doronicum cordatum* | Leopard's bane | *Hemerocallis* 'Hyperion' | 'Hyperion' daylily |
| *Elytrigia repens* | Quackgrass | *Hemerocallis* 'J. A. Crawford' | 'J. A. Crawford' daylily |
| *Epilobium angustifolium* | Fireweed | *Hemerocallis lilioasphodelus* | Lemon lily |
| *Epimedium grandiflorum* | Epimedium, longspur epimedium | *Hosta decorata* | Hosta |
| | | *Hosta sieboldiana* | Hosta |
| *Epimedium × versicolor* 'Sulphureum' | Epimedium, sulfur epimedium | *Hosta undulata* 'Thomas Hogg' | 'Thomas Hogg' hosta |
| *Epimedium × rubrum* | Epimedium, red epimedium | *Hyacinthoides hispanica* | Squill |
| *Equisetum arvense* | Common horsetail | *Hyacinthoides non-scripta* | English bluebell |
| *Equisetum telmateia* | Giant horsetail | *Hyacinthus orientalis* | Hyacinth |
| *Eranthus hyemalis* | Winter aconite | *Iris* 'Apricot Beauty' | 'Apricot Beauty' bearded iris |
| *Erica × darleyensis* 'Silberschmelze' | Mediterranean white heather | *Iris* 'Broadway Star' | 'Broadway Star' bearded iris |
| *Eruca vesicaria* subsp. *sativa* | Arugula | *Iris bucharica* | Jano iris |
| *Erysimum cheiri* | Wallflower | *Iris chrysographes* | Black iris |
| *Eucryphia × nymansensis* 'Nymansay' | 'Nymansay' eucryphia | *Iris danfordiae* | Danford iris |
| | | *Iris douglasiana* | Pacific Coast iris |
| *Euphorbia polychroma* | Polychrome euphorbia | *Iris foliosa* | Louisiana iris |
| *Fagus sylvatica* 'Atropunicea' | Copper beech, purple beech | *Iris forrestii* | Sino-Siberian iris |
| *Fagus sylvatica* 'Tricolor' | 'Tricolor' beech | *Iris graminea* | Spuria iris |
| *Filipendula carica* | Filipendula | *Iris* 'Great Lakes' | 'Great Lakes' bearded iris |
| *Filipendula rubra* 'Venusta' | 'Venusta' filipendula | *Iris innominata* | Oregon iris |
| *Foeniculum vulgare* | Fennel | *Iris kaempferi* | Japanese iris |
| *Fragaria vesca* 'Semperflorens' | Fraise du bois, alpine strawberry | *Iris* 'Maytime' | 'Maytime' bearded iris |
| | | *Iris missouriensis* | Western blue flag iris |
| *Fragaria vesca* 'Semperflorens Alba' | White fraise du bois | *Iris* 'Mulberry Rose' | 'Mulberry Rose' bearded iris |
| *Fragaria vesca* var. *bracteata* | Creeping strawberry | *Iris* 'New Snow' | 'New Snow' bearded iris |
| *Fragaria × ananassa* 'Quinault' | 'Quinault' strawberry | *Iris reticulata* | Reticulata iris |
| | | *Iris sibirica* | Siberian iris |
| *Fragaria × ananassa* 'Shuksan' | 'Shuksan' strawberry | *Iris tenax* | Toughleaf iris |
| | | *Iris unguicularis* | Algerian iris |
| *Fragaria × ananassa* 'Tri Star' | 'Tri Star' Strawberry | *Jasminum nudiflorum* | Winter jasmine |
| *Franklinia alatamaha* | Franklinia | *Kalmia latifolia* 'Alpine Pink' | 'Alpine Pink' mountain laurel |
| *Frtillaria camchatcensis* | Fritillaria, chocolate lily | | |
| *Fritillaria meleagris* | Fritillaria, checkered lily | *Lactuca sativa* 'Quatro Stagione' | 'Quatro Stagione' lettuce |
| *Fritillaria persica* | Persian fritillaria | *Lactuca sativa* 'Simpson's Elite' | 'Simpson's Elite' lettuce |
| *Galanthus elwesii* | Giant snowdrop | | |
| *Galanthus nivalis* | Snowdrop | *Lavandula angustifolia* | English lavender |
| *Gallium odoratum* | Sweet woodruff | *Leucojum vernum* | Leucojum, snowflake |
| *Garrya × issaquahensis* | Garrya | *Liatris spicata* | Liatris |
| *Gaultheria shallon* | Salal | *Ligularia dentata* | Ligularia |
| *Geranium himalayense* | Himalayan geranium | *Lilium* 'Casa Blanca' | 'Casa Blanca' lily |
| *Geranium* 'Johnson's Blue' | 'Johnson's Blue' geranium | *Lilium lancifolium* | Tiger lily |
| *Hedera helix* | English ivy | *Linaria purpurea* | Linaria, purple toadflax |

| | | | |
|---|---|---|---|
| *Lobelia erinus* | Lobelia | *Pisum sativum* | 'Oregon Trail' peas |
| *Lunaria annua* | Money plant, honesty | 'Oregon Trail' | |
| *Lychnis coronaria* | Raggedy robin | *Platanus × acerifolia* | London plane |
| *Lycopersicon esculentum* | 'Stupice' tomato | *Poa annuna* | Annual grass |
| 'Stupice' | | *Polygonatum biflorum* | True Solomon's seal |
| *Lysimachia clethroides* | Gooseneck lysimachia, | *Polystichum munitum* | Sword fern |
| | loose-strife | *Primula bulleyana* | Candelabra primula |
| *Lysimachia nummularia* | Creeping jenny | *Primula florinda* | Florinda primula |
| *Lythrum salicaria* | Lythrum | *Primula japonica* | Japanese primula |
| *Magnolia* 'Caerhayes Belle' | 'Caerhayes Belle' magnolia | *Primula vulgaris* | Primrose |
| *Magnolia campbellii* | 'Charles Raffill' magnolia | *Primula* 'Wanda' | 'Wanda' primrose |
| 'Charles Raffill' | | *Prunus armeniaca* 'Tilton' | 'Tilton' apricot |
| *Magnolia denudata* | Yulan magnolia | *Prunus × subhirtella* | 'Autumnalis' flowering |
| *Magnolia kobus* | Kobus magnolia | 'Autumnalis' | cherry |
| *Magnolia sieboldii* | Oyama magnolia | *Prunus × subhirtella* 'Rosea' | 'Whitcomb' flowering cherry |
| *Mahonia aquifolium* | Oregon grape | *Pseudotsuga taxifolia* | Douglas fir |
| *Malus domestica* | 'Gravenstein' apple | *Pulmonaia angustifolia* | Pulmonaria, lungwort |
| 'Gravenstein' | | *Pyrus communis* 'Bartlett' | 'Bartlett' pear |
| *Malus domestica* | 'Yellow Transparent' apple | *Ranunculus ficaria* | Lesser celandine |
| 'Yellow Transparent' | | *Rhododendron* 'Azor' | 'Azor' rhododendron |
| *Malus floribunda* | Flowering crabapple | *Rhododendron* 'Bow Bells' | 'Bow Bells' rhododendron |
| *Meconopsis cambrica* | Welsh poppy | *Rhododendron* 'Cilpinense' | 'Cilpinense' rhododendron |
| *Mentha requienii* | Corsican mint | *Rhododendron* 'Exbury | 'Exbury Hybrid' |
| *Mimulus guttatus* | Monkey-flower | Hybrid' | azalea |
| *Mirabilis jalapa* | Four o'clocks | *Rhododendron fortunei* | Fortunei rhododendron |
| *Montia perfoliato* | Miner's lettuce | *Rhododendron* 'Loderi | 'Loderi King George' |
| *Myosotis sylvatica* | Forget-me-not | King George' | rhododendron |
| *Narcissus bulbocodium* | Bulbocodium, | *Rhododendron* 'Loderi Pink | 'Loderi Pink Diamond' |
| | hoopskirt daffodil | Diamond' | rhododendron |
| *Narcissus jonquilla* | Jonquil | *Rhododendron* | 'Loderi Venus' |
| *Nicotiana alata* | Nicotiana | 'Loderi Venus' | rhododendron |
| *Nymphaea alba* | Water lily | *Rhododendron lutescens* | Sulfur rhododendron |
| *Nyssa sylvatica* | Nyssa, tupelo | 'Ashford' | 'Ashford' |
| *Ocimum basilicum* | Basil | *Rhododendron* 'Moonstone' | 'Moonstone' rhododendron |
| *Oenothera fruticosa* | Yellow evening primrose | *Rhododendron moupinense* | Moupinense rhododendron |
| *Oenothera speciosa* | Pink evening primrose | *Rhododendron* | Mucronulatum |
| 'Siskiyou' | | *mucronulatum* | rhododendron |
| *Omphalodes cappadocica* | Omphalodes | *Rhododendron* 'PJM' | 'PJM' rhododendron |
| *Ornithogalum arabicum* | Star of Bethlehem | *Rhododendron* 'Polar Bear' | 'Polar Bear' rhododendron |
| *Oxydendrum arboreum* | Oxydendrum | *Rhododendron* 'Praecox' | 'Praecox' rhododendron |
| *Paeonia suffruticoa* | | *Rhododendron viscistylum* | Viscistylum rhododendron |
| 'Oriental Pink' | 'Oriental Pink' tree peony | *Rhododendron* | Williamsianum |
| *Papaver rhoeas* | Shirley poppy | *williamsianum* | rhododendron |
| *Petroselinum crispum* | Parsley | *Ribes hirtellum* | Gooseberry |
| *Petunia × hybrida* | Petunia | *Ribes nigrum* | Black currant |
| *Phaseolus vulgaris* | 'Early Riser' pole bean | *Ribes rubrum* | Red currant |
| 'Early Riser' | | *Ribes sanguineum* | Pink flowering currant |
| *Phaseolus vulgaris* 'Primel' | Haricot vert bush bean | *Ribes sanguineum* 'King | 'King Edward VII' flowering |
| *Phlox paniculata* | Phlox | Edward VII' | currant |
| *Phlox paniculata* 'Mt. Fuji' | 'Mt. Fuji' phlox | *Ribes sanguineum* | 'White Icicle' flowering |
| *Phlox paniculata* 'Russian | | 'White Icicle' | currant |
| Violet' | 'Russian Violet' phlox | *Romneya coulteri* | Matilija poppy |
| *Phlox stolonifera* | Creeping phlox | *Rosa* 'Blanc Double de | 'Blanc Double de Coubert' |
| *Pinus sylvestris* | Scotch pine | Coubert' | rose |

| | |
|---|---|
| *Rosa* 'Bonica' | 'Bonica' rose |
| *Rosa eglanteria* | 'Eglantine' rose |
| *Rosa* 'Erfurt' | 'Erfurt' rose |
| *Rosa gallica versicolor* | 'Rosa Mundi' rose |
| *Rosa glauca* | Red leaf rose |
| *Rosa* 'Hanseat' | 'Hanseat' rose |
| *Rosa* 'Jacques Cartier' | 'Jacques Cartier' rose |
| *Rosa* 'La Marne' | 'La Marne' rose |
| *Rosa* 'Reine des Violettes' | 'Reine des Violettes' rose |
| *Rosa rugosa* | Rugosa rose |
| *Rosa rugosa* 'Frau Dagmar' | 'Frau Dagmar' rugosa rose |
| *Rosa* 'Sparrieshoop' | 'Sparrieshoop' rose |
| *Rosa spinosissima* | Scotch rose |
| *Rosa* 'Sutter's Gold' | 'Sutter's Gold' rose |
| *Rosa* 'Tausendschoen' | 'Tausendschoen' rose |
| *Rosa × odorata* 'Mutabilis' | 'Mutabilis' rose |
| *Rosmarinus officinalis* | Rosemary |
| *Rubus discolor* | Himalayan blackberry |
| *Rubus leucodemis* | Blackcap raspberry |
| *Rubus* 'Loganberry' | Loganberry |
| *Rubus* 'Marionberry' | Marionberry |
| *Salix caprea* | French pussy willow |
| *Salix melanostachys* | Black pussy willow |
| *Salpiglossis sinuata* | Salpiglossis, painted tongue |
| *Salvia officinalis* | Sage |
| *Sanguinaria canadensis* | Bloodroot |
| *Scilla siberica* | Siberian scilla |
| *Solanum tuberosum* 'Yellow Finn' | 'Yellow Finn' potato |
| *Soleirolia soleirolii* | Babies' tears |
| *Spinacia oleracea* 'Melody Hybrid' | 'Melody Hybrid' Spinach |
| *Stellaria media* | Chickweed |
| *Stewartia koreana* | Korean stewartia |
| *Stewartia monodelpha* | Tall stewartia |
| *Stewartia ovata* | Mountain stewartia |
| *Stewartia pseudocamellia* | Japanese stewartia |
| *Symphytum officinale* | Comfrey |
| *Tagetes patula* | French marigold |
| *Taraxacum officinale* | Dandelion |
| *Tellima grandiflora* | Fringecup |
| *Thalictrum aquilegifolium* | Meadow rue, thalictrum |
| *Thalictrum dipterocarpum* | Thalictrum |
| *Thalictrum rochebrunianum* | Thalictrum |
| *Trillium chloropetalum* var. *giganteum* | Black trillium |
| *Trillium ovatum* | Native trillium |
| *Tsuga heterophylla* | Western hemlock |
| *Urtica dioica* | Nettle |
| *Vacinium corymbosum* 'Bluecrop' | 'Bluecrop' blueberry |
| *Vacinium corymbosum* 'Dixie' | 'Dixie' blueberry |
| *Vancouveria chrysantha* | Vancouveria |
| *Vancouveria hexandra* | Vancouveria |
| *Verbena bonariensis* | Verbena bonariensis |
| *Viburnum × bodnantense* 'Dawn' | 'Dawn' viburnum |
| *Vicia faba* | Fava bean |
| *Viola labradorica* | Purple leaf violet |
| *Viola riviniana* | Pink violet |
| *Viola sororia* | Confederate violet |
| *Viola tricolor* | Johnny-jump-up |
| *Zantedeschia aethiopica* | Calla lily |
| *Zea mays* var. *rugosa* 'Early Choice' | 'Early Choice' sweet corn |
| *Zinnia angustifolia × elegans* 'Profusion Cherry' | 'Profusion Cherry' zinnia |
| *Zinnia elegans* | Zinnia |

# Plants Listed by Common Name

| Common name | Botanical name |
|---|---|
| Aconite, winter | *Eranthus hyemalis* |
| Anemone | |
|   Blanda, windflower | *Anemone blanda* |
|   Double white | *Anemone* 'Flore Pleno' |
|   Japanese | *Anemone × hybrida* 'Honorine Jobert' |
|   Wood | *Anemone nemorosa* |
| Apple | |
|   'Gravenstein' | *Malus domestica* 'Gravenstein' |
|   'Yellow Transparent' | *Malus domestica* 'Yellow Transparent' |
| Apricot, 'Tilton' | *Prunus armeniaca* 'Tilton' |
| Arabis | *Arabis caucasica* |
| Arugula | *Eruca vesicaria* subsp. *sativa* |
| Aster, pink | *Aster novae-angliae* |
| Astilbe | |
|   'Bridal Veil' | *Astilbe × arendsii* 'Bridal Veil' |
|   'Fanal' | *Astilbe* 'Fanal' |
|   'Ostrich Plume' | *Astilbe × arendsii* 'Ostrich Plume' |
| Aubrieta | *Aubrieta deltoidea* |
| Babies' tears | *Soleirolia soleirolii* |
| Basil (basilico) | *Ocimum basilicum* |
| Bean | |
|   Bush, haricot vert | *Phaseolus vulgaris* 'Primel' |
|   Fava | *Vicia faba* |
|   Pole, 'Early Riser' | *Phaseolus vulgaris* 'Early Riser' |
| Beech | |
|   Copper | *Fagus sylvatica* 'Atropunicea' |
|   Purple | *Fagus sylvatica* 'Atropunicea' |
|   'Tricolor' | *Fagus sylvatica* 'Tricolor' |
| Beet, 'Detroit Dark Red' | *Beta vulgaris* 'Detroit Dark Red' |
| Blackberry, Himalayan | *Rubus discolor* |
| Blackcap | *Rubus leucodemis* |
| Bloodroot | *Sanguinaria canadensis* |
| Bluebell, English | *Hyacinthoides non-scripta* |
| Blueberry | |
|   'Bluecrop' | *Vaccinium corymbosum* 'Bluecrop' |
|   'Dixie' | *Vaccinium corymbosum* 'Dixie' |
| Camass | *Camassia cusickii* |
| Camass | *Camassia quamash* |
| Camellia | |
|   'Briar rose' | *Camellia sasanqua* 'Briar Rose' |
|   'Finlandia' | *Camellia japonica* 'Finlandia' |
|   'Howard Asper' | *Camellia japonica* 'Howard Asper' |
|   Japanese | *Camellia japonica* |
|   Sasanqua | *Camellia sasanqua* |
|   'Vericolor' | *Camellia sasanqua* 'Vericolor' |
| Campanula | |
|   Canterbury bells | *Campanula medium* |
|   Dwarf, harebell | *Campanula rotundifolia* |
| Carnation | *Dianthus caryophyllus* |
| Carpenteria | *Carpenteria californica* |
| Celandine | |
|   Greater | *Chelidonium majus* |
|   Lesser | *Ranunculus ficaria* |
| Cherry | |
|   Cornelian | *Cornus mas* |
|   Flowering, 'Autumnalis' | *Prunus × subhirtella* 'Autumnalis' |
|   Flowering, 'Whitcomb' | *Prunus × subhirtella* 'Rosea' |
|   Flowering, 'Yoshino' | *Prunus × yedoensis* |
| Chickweed | *Stellaria media* |
| Chionodoxa | *Chionodoxa luciliae* |
| Chives | *Allium schoenoprasum* |
| Clematis | |
|   Montana | *Clematis montana* |
|   Wild | *Clematis vitalba* |
| Cleome | *Cleome hasslerana* |
| Columbine | *Aquilegia* hybrids |
| Comfrey | *Symphytum officinale* |
| Coptis | *Coptis trifolia* |
| Corn, 'Early Choice' sweet | *Zea mays* var. *rugosa* 'Early Choice' |
| Cosmos | *Cosmos bipinnatus* |
| Crapapple, flowering | *Malus floribunda* |
| Creeping jenny | *Lysimachia nummularia* |
| Crocus, tomasinianus | *Crocus tomasinianus* |
| Cucumber | *Cucumis sativus* |
| Currant | |
|   Black | *Ribes nigrum* |
|   Flowering, 'King Edward VII' | *Ribes sanguineum* 'King Edward VII' |
|   Flowering, pink | *Ribes sanguineum* |
|   Flowering, 'White Icicle' | *Ribes sanguineum* 'White Icicle' |
|   Red | *Ribes rubrum* |
| Cyclamen | *Cyclamen coum* |
| Cyclamen | *Cyclamen hederifolium* |
| Cypress, Italian | *Cupressus sempervirens* 'Stricta' |
| Daffodil, hoopskirt | *Narcissus bulbocodium* |
| Daisy, Shasta | *Chrysanthemum maximum* |

| | | | |
|---|---|---|---|
| Dandelion | *Taraxacum officinale* | Harebells | *Campanula rotundifolia* |
| Daphne, winter | *Daphne odora* | Heather, | *Erica × darleyensis* |
| Daylily | | Mediterranean white | 'Silberschmelze" |
| 'Big Boy Bubba' | *Hemerocallis* 'Big Boy Bubba' | Helenium | *Helenium autumnale* |
| 'Coleman's Dream' | *Hemerocallis* 'Coleman's Dream' | Heliotrope | *Heliotropium arborescens* |
| | | Honesty | *Lunaria annua* |
| 'Hyperion' | *Hemerocallis* 'Hyperion' | Horse and rider | *Arisaema triphyllum* |
| 'J. A. Crawford' | *Hemerocallis* 'J. A. Crawford' | Horsetail | |
| Dill | *Anethum graveolens* | Common | *Equisetum arvense* |
| Dogwood | | Giant | *Equisetum telmateia* |
| Cornelian cherry | *Cornus mas* | Hosta | *Hosta decorata* |
| Eastern | *Cornus florida* | Hosta | *Hosta sieboldiana* |
| 'Eddie's White Wonder' | *Cornus* 'Eddie's White Wonder' | Hosta, 'Thomas Hogg' | *Hosta undulata* 'Thomas Hogg' |
| Redtwig | *Cornus stolonifera* | Hyacinth | *Hyacinthus orientalis* |
| Western | *Cornus nuttallii* | Iris | |
| Elderberry | *Sambucus racemosa* | Algerian | *Iris unguicularis* |
| Endive, curly | *Cichorium endivia* | Bearded, 'Apricot Beauty' | *Iris* 'Apricot Beauty' |
| Epimedium | | Bearded, 'Broadway Star' | *Iris* 'Broadway Star' |
| Longspur | *Epimedium grandiflorum* | Bearded, 'Great Lakes' | *Iris* 'Great Lakes' |
| Red | *Epimedium × rubrum* | Bearded, 'Maytime' | *Iris* 'Maytime' |
| Sulfur | *Epimedium × versicolor* 'Sulphureum' | Bearded, 'Mulberry Rose' | *Iris* 'Mulberry Rose' |
| Eucryphia, 'Nymansay' | *Eucryphia × nymansensis* 'Nymansay' | Bearded, 'New Snow' | *Iris* 'New Snow' |
| | | Black | *Iris chrysographes* |
| Euphorbia, polychome | *Euphorbia polychroma* | Danford | *Iris danfordiae* |
| Fennel | *Foeniculum vulgare* | Flag, western blue | *Iris missouriensis* |
| Fern, sword | *Polystichum munitum* | Jano | *Iris bucharica* |
| Feverfew | *Chrysanthemum parthenium* | Japanese | *Iris kaempferi* |
| Filipendula | *Filipendula carica* | Louisiana | *Iris foliosa* |
| Filipendula, 'Venusta' | *Filipendula rubra* 'Venusta' | Oregon | *Iris innominata* |
| Fir, Douglas | *Pseudotsuga taxifolia* | Pacific Coast | *Iris douglasiana* |
| Fireweed | *Epilobium angustifolium* | Reticulata | *Iris reticulata* |
| Forget-me-not | *Myosotis sylvatica* | Siberian | *Iris sibirica* |
| Four o'clocks | *Mirabilis jalapa* | Sino-Siberian | *Iris forrestii* |
| Foxglove | *Digitalis purpurea* | Spuria | *Iris graminea* |
| Fraise du bois | *Fragaria vesca* 'Semperflorens' | Toughleaf | *Iris tenax* |
| Fraise du bois, white | *Fragaria vesca* 'Semperflorens Alba' | Ivy, English | *Hedera helix* |
| | | Jack-in-the-pulpit | *Arisaema triphyllum* |
| Franklinia | *Franklinia alatamaha* | Jasmine, winter | *Jasminum nudiflorum* |
| Fringecup | *Tellima grandiflora* | Johnny-jump-up | *Viola tricolor* |
| Fritillaria, checkered lily | *Fritillaria meleagris* | Jonquil | *Narcissus jonquilla* |
| Fritillaria, chocolate lily | *Fritillaria camchatcensis* | Kinnikinnick | *Arctostaphylos uva-ursi* |
| Fritillaria, Persian | *Fritillaria persica* | Larkspur | *Consolida ajacis* |
| Garrya | *Garrya × issaquahensis* | Laurel, mountain, | *Kalmia latifolia* |
| Geranium | | 'Alpine Pink' | 'Alpine Pink' |
| Himalayan | *Geranium himalayense* | Lavender, English | *Lavandula angustifolia* |
| 'Johnson's Blue' | *Geranium* 'Johnson's Blue' | Lenten rose | *Helleborus orientalis* |
| Goat's beard | *Aruncus dioicus* | Leopard's bane | *Doronicum cordatum* |
| Golden thread | *Coptis trifolia* | Lettuce | |
| Gooseberry | *Ribes hirtellum* | Miner's | *Montia perfoliata* |
| Grape, Oregon | *Mahonia aquifolium* | 'Quatro Stagione' | *Lactuca sativa* 'Quatro Stagione' |
| Grass, annual | *Poa annuna* | | |
| Grass, quack | *Elytrigia repens* | 'Simpson's Elite' | *Lactuca sativa* 'Simpson's Elite' |

| | |
|---|---|
| Leucojum | *Leucojum vernum* |
| Liatris | *Liatris spicata* |
| Ligularia | *Ligularia dentata* |
| Lily | |
| Calla | *Zantedeschia aethiopica* |
| 'Casa Blanca' | *Lilium* 'Casa Blanca' |
| Checkered | *Fritillaria meleagris* |
| Chocolate | *Frilillaria camchatcensis* |
| Lemon | *Hemerocallis lilioasphodelus* |
| Tiger | *Lilium lancifolium* |
| Water | *Nymphaea alba* |
| Lily-of-the-valley | *Convallaria majalis* |
| Linaria | *Linaria purpurea* |
| Lobelia | *Lobelia erinus* |
| Loganberry | *Rubus* 'Loganberry' |
| Loosestrife, gooseneck | *Lysimachia clethroides* |
| Lythrum | *Lythrum salicaria* |
| Magnolia | |
| 'Caerhayes Belle' | *Magnolia* 'Caerhayes Belle' |
| 'Charles Raffill' | *Magnolia campbellii* 'Charles Raffill' |
| Kobus | *Magnolia kobus* |
| Oyama | *Magnolia sieboldii* |
| Yulan | *Magnolia denudata* |
| Maiden, pink | *Dianthus deltoides* |
| Manzanita | |
| Manzanita, hairy | *Arctostaphylos columbiana* |
| Monterey manzanita | *Arctostaphylos hookeri* |
| Maple | |
| Big leaf | *Acer macrophyllum* |
| Vine | *Acer circinatum* |
| Marigold | |
| French | *Tagetes patula* |
| Marsh | *Caltha palustris* |
| Marionberry | *Rubus* 'Marionberry' |
| Mint, Corsican | *Mentha requienii* |
| Money plant | *Lunaria annua* |
| Monkey-flower | *Mimulus guttatus* |
| Monkshood | *Aconitum napellus* |
| Morning glory | *Calystegia sepium* |
| Naked ladies | *Amaryllis belladonna* |
| Nettle | *Urtica dioica* |
| Nicotiana | *Nicotiana alata* |
| Nyssa | *Nyssa sylvatica* |
| Omphalodes | *Omphalodes cappadocica* |
| Onion | |
| Egyptian, walking | *Allium cepa* var. *viviparum* |
| Red | *Allium cepa* |
| 'Walla Walla Sweet' | *Allium cepa* 'Walla Walla Sweet' |
| Oxydendrum | *Oxydendrum arboreum* |
| Painted tongue | *Salpiglossis sinuata* |
| Parsley | *Petroselinum crispum* |
| Pear, 'Bartlett' | *Pyrus communis* 'Bartlett' |

| | |
|---|---|
| Peas, 'Oregon Trail' | *Pisum sativum* 'Oregon Trail' |
| Peony, tree, 'Oriental Pink' | *Paeonia suffruticosa* 'Oriental Pink' |
| Pepper | |
| 'Hungarian Red' | *Capsicum annuum* 'Hungarian Red' |
| 'Hungarian Yellow' | *Capsicum annuum* 'Hungarian Yellow' |
| Petunia | *Petunia* × *hybrida* |
| Phlox | *Phlox paniculata* |
| Creeping | *Phlox stolonifera* |
| 'Mt. Fuji' | *Phlox paniculata* 'Mt. Fuji' |
| 'Russian Violet' | *Phlox paniculata* 'Russian Violet' |
| Pine, Scotch | *Pinus sylvestris* |
| Plane, London | *Platanus* × *acerifolia* |
| Poppy | |
| Matilija | *Romneya coulteri* |
| Shirley | *Papaver rhoeas* |
| Welsh | *Meconopsis cambrica* |
| Potato, 'Yellow Finn' | *Solanum tuberosum* 'Yellow Finn' |
| Primrose | |
| Evening, pink | *Oenothera speciosa* 'Siskiyou' |
| Evening, yellow | *Oenothera fruticosa* |
| Common | *Primula vulgaris* |
| 'Wanda' | *Primula* 'Wanda' |
| Primula | |
| Candelabra | *Primula bulleyana* |
| Florinda | *Primula florinda* |
| Japanese | *Primula japonica* |
| Pulmonaria, lungwort | *Pulmonaria angustifolia* |
| Pussy willow | |
| Black | *Salix melanostachys* |
| French | *Salix caprea* |
| Quackgrass | *Elytrigia repens* |
| Quince | |
| Flowering, 'Nivalis' | *Chaenomeles speciosa* 'Nivalis' |
| Flowering, 'Snow Queen' | *Chaenomeles japonica* 'Snow Queen' |
| Raggedy robin | *Lychnis coronaria* |
| Rape | *Brassica napus* |
| Raspberry, blackcap | *Rubus leucodemis* |
| Rhododendron | |
| 'Azor' | *Rhododendron* 'Azor' |
| 'Bow Bells' | *Rhododendron* 'Bow Bells' |
| 'Cilpinense' | *Rhododendron* 'Cilpinense' |
| 'Exbury Hybrid' | *Rhododendron* 'Exbury Hybrid' |
| Fortunei | *Rhododendron fortunei* |
| 'Loderi King George' | *Rhododendron* 'Loderi King George' |

'Loderi Pink Diamond'   *Rhododendron* 'Loderi Pink Diamond'

|  |  |
|---|---|
| 'Loderi Pink Diamond' | *Rhododendron* 'Loderi Pink Diamond' |
| 'Loderi Venus' | *Rhododendron* 'Loderi Venus' |
| 'Moonstone' | *Rhododendron* 'Moonstone' |
| Moupinense | *Rhododendron moupinense* |
| Mucronulatum | *Rhododendron mucronulatum* |
| 'PJM' | *Rhododendron* 'PJM' |
| 'Polar Bear' | *Rhododendron* 'Polar Bear' |
| 'Praecox' | *Rhododendron* 'Praecox' |
| Sulfur | *Rhododendron lutescens* 'Ashford' |
| Viscistylum | *Rhododendron viscistylum* |
| Williamsianum | *Rhododendron williamsianum* |
| Rockcress | *Arabis caucasica* |
| Rockrose, white | *Cistus × hybridus* |
| Rose | |
|   'Blanc Double de Coubert' | *Rosa* 'Blanc Double de Coubert' |
|   'Bonica' | *Rosa* 'Bonica' |
|   'Eglantine' | *Rosa eglanteria* |
|   'Erfurt' | *Rosa* 'Erfurt' |
|   'Frau Dagmar' | *Rosa rugosa* 'Frau Dagmar' |
|   'Hanseat' | *Rosa* 'Hanseat' |
|   'Jacques Cartier' | *Rosa* 'Jacques Cartier' |
|   'La Marne' | *Rosa* 'La Marne' |
|   Lenten | *Helleborus orientalis* |
|   'Mutabilis' | *Rosa × odorata* 'Mutabilis' |
|   Red leaf | *Rosa glauca* |
|   'Reine des Violettes' | *Rosa* 'Reine des Violettes' |
|   'Rosa Mundi' | *Rosa gallica versicolor* |
|   Rugosa | *Rosa rugosa* |
|   Scotch | *Rosa spinosissima* |
|   'Sparrieshoop' | *Rosa* 'Sparrieshoop' |
|   'Sutter's Gold' | *Rosa* 'Sutter's Gold' |
|   'Tausendschoen' | *Rosa* 'Tausendschoen' |
| Rosemary | *Rosmarinus officinalis* |
| Rue, meadow | *Thalictrum aquilegifolium* |
| Sage | *Salvia officinalis* |
| Salal | *Gaultheria shallon* |
| Salpiglossis | *Salpiglossis sinuata* |
| Scilla, Siberian | *Scilla siberica* |
| Shallot | *Allium oschaninii* |
| Snowdrop | |
|   Giant | *Galanthus elwesii* |
|   Snowdrop | *Galanthus nivalis* |
| Snowflake | *Leucojum vernum* |
| Solomon's seal, true | *Polygonatum biflorum* |
| Spinach, 'Melody Hybrid' | *Spinacia oleracea* 'Melody Hybrid' |
| Squill | *Hyacinthoides hispanica* |
| Star of Bethleham | *Ornithogalum arabicum* |
| Stewartia | |
|   Japanese | *Stewartia pseudocamellia* |
|   Korean | *Stewartia koreana* |
|   Mountain | *Stewartia ovata* |
|   Tall stewartia | *Stewartia monodelpha* |
| Strawberry | |
|   Alpine | *Fragaria vesca* |
|   Creeping | *Fragaria vesca* var. *bracteata* |
|   Fraise du bois | *Fragaria vesca* 'Semperflorens' |
|   Fraise du bois, white | *Fragaria vesca* 'Semperflorens Alba' |
|   'Quinault' | *Fragaria × ananassa* 'Quinault' |
|   'Shuksan' | *Fragaria × ananassa* 'Shuksan' |
|   'Tri Star' | *Fragaria × ananassa* 'Tri Star' |
| Sunrose | *Helianthemum nummularium* |
|   'Wisley Pink' | *Helianthemum* 'Wisley Pink' |
| Swiss chard | |
|   'Fordhook Giant' | *Beta vulgaris* 'Fordhook Giant' |
|   'Vulcan' | *Beta vulgaris* 'Vulcan' |
| Thalictrum | *Thalictrum aquilegifolium* |
| Thalictrum | *Thalictrum dipterocarpum* |
| Thalictrum | *Thalictrum rochebrunianum* |
| Thistle | *Cirsium arvense* |
| Toadflax, purple | *Linaria purpurea* |
| Tomato, 'Stupice' | *Lycopersicum esculentum* 'Stupice' |
| Trillium | |
|   Black | *Trillium chloropetalum* var. *giganteum* |
|   Native | *Trillium ovatum* |
| Vancouveria | |
|   Evergreen | *Vancouveria chrysantha* |
|   Vancouveria | *Vancouveria hexandra* |
| Verbena | *Verbena bonariensis* |
| Viburnum, 'Dawn' | *Viburnum × bodnantense* 'Dawn' |
| Violet | |
|   Confederate | *Viola sororia* |
|   Johnny-jump-up | *Viola tricolor* |
|   Pink | *Viola riviniana* |
|   Purple leaf | *Viola labradorica* |
| Wallflower | *Erysimum cheiri* |
| Washington thorn | *Crataegus phaenopyrum* |
| Wind flower | *Anemone blanda* |
| Winter hazel | |
|   Buttercup | *Corylopsis pauciflora* |
|   Spike | *Corylopsis spicata* |
| Wintersweet | *Chimonanthus praecox* |
| Woodruff, sweet | *Gallium odoratum* |
| Zinnia | |
|   'Profusion Cherry' | *Zinnia angustifolia × elegans* 'Profusion Cherry' |
|   Zinnia | *Zinnia elegans* |
| Zucchini | *Cucurbita pepo* |

# Photographic Credits and Acknowledgments

The database and Web site are by Benjamin Streissguth. All drawings are by Daniel Streissguth. All photographs are by the authors, with the following exceptions:

WILL AUSTIN  Figures 3.6, 3.8, 3.13, 3.14, 4.6, 4.11, 5.5, 7.3, 7.12, 9.7, 9.10, and pages ii, v

DAVID BARNES  Figure 2.15

VICTOR GARDAYA  Figure 2.5

MICHAEL GRAVES  Figures 2.20, 2.21, 3.4, 3.19, 5.9, 6.3, 7.6

STEVEN REEVES  Figure 5.10

SEATTLE MUNICIPAL ARCHIVES PHOTO COLLECTION, NO. 5916  Figure 1.9

The authors are grateful to individuals who have been splendid advisors to us in the preparation of this book. At the University of Washington Press, we thank especially Naomi Pascal, former associate director and editor-in-chief, who championed the idea of this book from the start and made sure it became a reality; Pat Soden, director; Marilyn Trueblood, managing editor; Gretchen Van Meter, copyeditor; and Thomas Eykemans, designer. At the Arboretum Foundation, Neal Lessenger, past interim executive director and chairman of the board, has also been a staunch supporter of the project.

# About the Authors

ANN STREISSGUTH is professor emerita, Department of Psychiatry and Behavioral Sciences, School of Medicine, University of Washington. She founded and is the former director of the Fetal Alcohol and Drug Unit, University of Washington.

DANIEL STREISSGUTH is professor emeritus and former chair, Department of Architecture, College of Architecture and Urban Planning, University of Washington.

BENJAMIN STREISSGUTH received a bachelor of landscape architecture degree from the University of Washington. He also holds applied technical arts degrees in Horticultural Design, Horticultural Maintenance, and Horticultural Installation, plus a Certificate of Ornamental Horticulture, from Edmonds Community College.

DOUGLAS KELBAUGH is professor and former dean of the Taubman College of Architecture and Urban Planning, University of Michigan. He is the former chair of the Department of Architecture at the University of Washington.

# Index

Page numbers in bold represent photographs. All plant names are listed in the form(s) in which they appear in the text; see also common and botanical names listed in Appendix 3.